HOPEFUL SORROW

HOPEFUL SORROW

Turning to God in Hope
When Childhood Wounds
Have You Turning Away

JULIE BUSLER

PUBLISHING®
BRENTWOOD, TENNESSEE

Copyright © 2025 by Julie Busler
All rights reserved.
Printed in the United States of America

9-798-3845-1733-7

Published by B&H Publishing Group
Brentwood, Tennessee

Dewey Decimal Classification: 234.2
Subject Heading: HOPE \ JOY AND
SORROW \ CHRISTIAN LIVING

Unless otherwise noted, all Scripture is taken from the Christian Standard Bible, copyright © 2017 by Holman Bible Publishers. Used by permission. Christian Standard Bible®, and CSB® are federally registered trademarks of Holman Bible Publishers, all rights reserved.

Scripture references marked ESV are taken from English Standard Version. ESV® Text Edition: 2016. Copyright © 2001 by Crossway Bibles, a publishing ministry of Good News Publishers.

Scripture references marked NIV are taken from New International Version®, NIV® Copyright ©1973, 1978, 1984, 2011 by Biblica, Inc.® Used by permission. All rights reserved worldwide.

Scripture references marked AMP are taken from the Amplified Bible, copyright © 2015 by The Lockman Foundation, La Habra, CA 90631. All rights reserved.

Scripture references marked AMPC are taken from the Amplified Bible, Classic Edition, Copyright © 1954, 1958, 1962, 1964, 1965, 1987 by The Lockman Foundation.

Scripture references marked NKJV are taken from the New Kings James Version® copyright © 1982 by Thomas Nelson. Used by permission. All rights reserved.

Front cover design and illustration by David Wardle.
Author photo by Meshali Mitchell.

1 2 3 4 5 6 • 28 27 26 25

To my future grandchildren and great-grandchildren.
Breaking cycles is hard, but you are worth it.
I love you already.

This book is for informational purposes only and is not a substitute for professional medical or mental health advice. Always consult your doctor or a licensed professional regarding your health.

If you are experiencing thoughts of self-harm or suicide, seek help immediately. Call or text the Suicide & Crisis Lifeline at 988, call 911, or go to your nearest emergency room.

Here are some additional protective actions you can take as you read this book:

1. **Talk to a Trusted Friend, Family Member, or Pastor:** Share your thoughts, feelings, and struggles with someone supportive and compassionate.
2. **Journal:** Write down your thoughts to process emotions.
3. **Read Alongside a Therapist:** Read and discuss this book with a counselor for personalized care and support.
4. **Practice Self-Care:** Engage in activities that reduce stress and honor God as a way to promote well-being.
5. **Stay Connected to Community:** Avoid isolation by maintaining connections with supportive people, and participating in church activities.
6. **Create a Safety Plan:** Work with a professional to develop a plan for managing difficult emotions or crises.
7. **Limit Access to Harmful Tools:** Make your environment safe by removing self-harm means.
8. **Pray and Seek God's Guidance:** Bring your struggles to God in prayer and lean on His strength.
9. **Read at Your Own Pace:** Take your time reading this book and processing what you learn.
10. **Read the Bible:** While this book is intended to encourage your faith, it is no replacement for the Word of God.

Contents

Introduction: Finally Honest 1

PART 1: LAMENT

Chapter 1: Permission to Grieve. 11
Chapter 2: What Is Lament. 25
Chapter 3: Practicing Lament 45

PART 2: HINDRANCES TO LAMENT

Chapter 4: Emotional Neglect. 63
Chapter 5: Attachment 77
Chapter 6: Fear of Abandonment 99
Chapter 7: Faithful Love 115
Chapter 8: Breaking the Cycle. 131
Chapter 9: Penitential Lament. 147

PART 3: IMPLICATIONS FOR THE CHURCH

Chapter 10: Lamenting Together. 163
Chapter 11: Missional Lament. 177
Epilogue: Remembering with Grace 193

Acknowledgments 199
Appendix 1: Words to Help You Lament. 201
Appendix 2: Reflection Prompts 203
Bibliography. 205
Notes 213

Joy HAS LEFT
OUR HEARTS;
OUR *dancing*
HAS TURNED
TO *mourning*.

LAMENTATIONS 5:15

INTRODUCTION

Finally Honest

My therapist once told me she's had clients anxiously pick at the couch's green velvet seat buttons until popping them off altogether, and this time I stopped my fidgety fingers just short of being added to this statistic. We were discussing my past, and as if out of nowhere, "I just don't want this story anymore" flew out of mouth, interrupting her with a fiery passion. Hearing my feelings out loud was uncomfortable, to say the least. As I glanced up at her, unsure of how she would react, tears blurred her face.

I hated my story, but voicing that deeply felt frustration felt foreign. Like a shaken-up soda can, I exploded when her questions opened me up. Tumbling into a dark hole of embarrassment, I realized she wasn't reacting like I thought she would. She calmly and compassionately looked at me, allowing my words to overtake the wisdom she was sharing, and held space for me to love God while simultaneously not loving my story.

There was no correction, because no correction was needed.

I didn't understand at the time, but that moment in therapy became a turning point in learning to turn toward God in my grief. Hearing my confession felt like two steps back, but in hindsight, I was running full speed ahead toward healing. You can't heal from that which you refuse to deal with, and to deal with something, you must first admit it.

As a chronic pretender, or performer you might say, she saw my honest pain rather than my persona. I wanted my insides to match my outsides, but that cognitive dissonance was a learned behavior programmed in childhood. Yes, I had started living a more authentic life after a few years of working with her; however, there was still an element of secrecy I felt enslaved to—secrecy with God, even though I believed He knows the thoughts of man (Ps. 94:11). Because I believed that true faith wouldn't look at the Most High and express hatred for the circumstances His sovereignty allowed, my words felt wrong. I felt wrong.

But wrong beliefs can be unlearned, and while emotions are a gift to be celebrated, they can make things appear contrary to the truth. Proverbs 16:25 says, "There is a way that seems right to a person, but its end is the way to death." The path of pretending to be at peace with my story seemed right, but this was leading me toward death. Not eternal death, for I was a child of God, but the death of authentic relationships, death of inner peace, death of flourishing securely with God, death of my fruitfulness, and even physical death because my hidden pain was making that option more appealing with each year that slipped by.

But why do we live as though protesting our confusing and difficult circumstances to the God we love and trust is frowned upon at best, unholy at worst? The Bible is teeming with protests from the faithful, including Jesus himself. Pretending to love your horrific story is not holy. Holiness is seen in submitting to God even when you wish your story was different, for it was Jesus who famously prayed in the garden, "Father, if you are willing, take this cup away from me—nevertheless, not my will, but yours, be done" (Luke 22:42).

But how can you submit to God, or rather accept and yield to Him as the author of your days, and still have the ability to tell Him you don't like His plan? What I've come to believe is that submission and silence are not mutually exclusive. You can accept God's plan and yet still tell Him the agony you feel within it.

A cathartic release happened through my confession in that dimly lit counseling office nestled in the heart of Oklahoma City. Putting voice to my anguish meant my therapist bore witness to my pain, challenging the isolation I felt within it. It was as though she linked arms with me in my sorrow, showing me the sweetness found in lamenting pain and confusion in the context of Christian community. This created a healthy attachment to her which challenged the unhealthy attachments from my childhood, helping me learn with wobbly legs that security with fellow believers can transfer to security with the Father. In her presence, I acknowledged my once deeply covered emotion that seemed in opposition to the promises of God, which meant I had taken the first baby steps in emerging from it. Her maturity of faith coupled with her applause of my authenticity caused me to pause and consider the goodness of my lament rather than the shame in it. Not only did God know my struggle, He invited me to cry out in it, to call it what it is.

As I've pondered that moment, I've also thought about the hard, sometimes confusing stories of the faithful that we all know and love in the Bible. I imagine Abraham didn't want to sacrifice Isaac. I know Moses didn't want to leave his mother who nursed him, and surely her heart shattered as he left. I know Job hated his children dying. Hannah's infertility caused her distress. Naomi deeply grieved losing her husband and sons. I'm positive Noah was distraught at the sound of people drowning. There is no way Esther loved being orphaned. While courageous, surely Daniel didn't enjoy being thrown in with lions. How could Mary Magdalene have liked being possessed by demons? There is no way Paul loved the multiple shipwrecks in his story. And I can't imagine John loving his exile.

Many of our Bible heroes offer gut-wrenching laments throughout Scripture, such as Naomi who lamented by saying, "Don't call me Naomi.... Instead, call me Mara, for the Almighty has made life very bitter for me. I went away full, but the LORD has brought me home empty. Why call me Naomi when the LORD has caused me to suffer and the Almighty has sent such tragedy upon me?" (Ruth 1:20–21 NLT). Her words expressed faith, for if she believed God had truly abandoned her, she would not have ventured back to Bethlehem in search of the provision she heard He was pouring out on His people. She spoke truthfully about God, acknowledging His control of all things. She didn't turn away from Him in the midst of her bitter grief, but rather moved toward Him as she went to Bethlehem. And miraculously, she didn't hide her trauma, and it was her bereft condition that led the women in Bethlehem to ask in shock, "Can this be Naomi?" (v. 19).

It's Naomi's story that leads me back to my own. I left for the mission field of Turkey at the age of thirty, beaming with joy, only to return to Oklahoma, begging for death after a harrowing hospitalization in a Turkish psychiatric hospital. Suicidality had stolen my ability to pretend my pain didn't exist. I imagine those who saw me wondered, "Can this be Julie?"

Before Naomi made the trip back to Bethlehem, her husband and both sons died, and one of her two daughters-in-law left her to return back to her home and gods. Naomi knew overwhelming loss, and like her, loss seemed to overwhelm me. I don't love that my mom died from cancer. Emotional neglect by a dad who died by suicide feels unfair. I still struggle with the birth trauma that ushered in my new calling as a mother. I hate that I shoved the sorrow down and pretended I was okay because I didn't realize I could voice it. And I can still feel confused as to how a good Father could let this all happen. The repercussions of unresolved grief have been extreme, certainly playing a part in the suicidal ideation that took over my mind for decades. However, through a careful study of Scripture, as well as utilizing resources such as evidence-based therapy, which I believe to be a common grace from God, I have found healing and hope in the most unlikely of places: *lament*.

Lament is "a crying out in grief,"[1] and just like grief, lament is not tame. It can be wild in its wailing or weeping, complaining or mourning aloud, but it comes back to a place of hope and trust in the character of God. Lament is the hopeful song sung in the dark night of the soul suspended between our permitted pain and the promises of God. It's a grace of God given to us in the midst of the *already* and the *not yet*. It's voicing the heart's pain while waiting to see its purpose. Believers lament because life can often present in opposition to our God who is good. When circumstances appear to clash with God's promises, lament is an invitation for struggling children of God to keep calling on their Father to do something, to act on their behalf. Sorrow is expected during our sojourn on earth; however, when hope marries sorrow, you see a godly lamenter who is steadfast in seeking God's answers and help when action on His part seems delayed.

For me, it has taken a messy journey through grief to see my need for lament, and the moment God revealed to me that I was finally understanding this important song of sorrow happened to be on that same green couch in my therapist's office. As one who was emotionally ill-equipped and delayed in navigating the wilderness of grief, my therapist often interjected phrases into our conversations like, "This is grief," to help me recognize its presence.

When I cried and complained that I didn't have a mom, she said, "This is grief."

When I expressed how life isn't what I expected, she said, "This is grief."

When I was angry that my dad chose to die, she said gently, "This is grief."

The more I recognized grief, the more confronted I was by my lack of understanding in how to grieve in a godly way. An honest way. A hopeful way. Until one day when God gave me a real-life moment of learning what He had already been opening my eyes to in Scripture: *lament*. I arrived at therapy with a tender heart that had tumbled back into being acutely aware of my grief through being triggered. I sat on her couch and exclaimed through tears, "How long will it feel this way?" And although not explicitly stated, my settled belief in the sovereignty of God implied my cry was directed toward Him. My anguished question was immediately interrupted by the Spirit's clarity. I sat straight up and said, "This is lament." I was practically learning, yet not quite absorbing, what the Lord would eventually place on my heart to share with you. That moment in front of my therapist wouldn't be the last when my frustrated cries in her office would be highlighted by the Spirit as lament.

I can assure you that I have lived sorrow—I still do every day—but I can say with certainty that the gift of lament is a lifeline. Your sorrow may persist, but there is a hopeful way to turn to the Father in the midst of it, because that's what lament is—a turning. Depression may seemingly take your face in its hands as if to say, "Look at me," but lament is choosing not to cooperate. Lament is fighting the temptation to turn away in despair by turning toward the Father who rescues you because He delights in you (Ps. 18:19). The depression may persist, but your focus on God offers hope in the midst of that pain.

And that is what we all long for: hope in our sorrow.

Lament gives dignity to our suffering and fosters attachment to the God you love in the midst of a story you don't. Your grief is not meaningless, for it's through sorrow that we learn lessons that aren't learned any other way. Even the psalmist said, "Before I was afflicted I went astray, but now I keep your word" (Ps. 119:67). Through the Lord, the unwanted experience of grief can be the most beautiful gift hidden within black wrapping paper. What may appear to be delay on God's part is working for your good; however, because He knows the pain of waiting, He invites you to lament. And through lament, we join those in the Bible with difficult stories whose pain was a pathway to grasp who God really is.

Abraham learned his God provides. Moses learned his God delivers. Job learned his God controls all things. Hannah learned her God hears prayers. Naomi learned her God redeems. Noah learned his God saves. Esther learned her God is sovereign. Daniel learned his God protects. Mary Magdalene learned her God heals. Paul learned his God strengthens. John learned his God wins.

And I have learned that God is the God of hope.

Pain and hope coexist in believers, for pain highlights the sustaining power of hope in Christ, and hope fosters endurance in the midst of pain. And right there in the middle is where you find lament. If you resonate with David who once said, "How long, Lord? Will you forget me forever? How long will you hide your face from me? How long will I store up anxious concerns within me, agony in my mind every day?" (Ps. 13:1–2a), I hope you'll continue on this journey with me of learning to lament while also considering what may be hindering you from practicing it. And may you one day say alongside other sorrowful, yet hopeful saints, "But I have trusted in your faithful love; my heart will rejoice in your deliverance. I will sing to the Lord because he has treated me generously" (vv. 5–6).

PART 1
Lament

CHAPTER 1

Permission to Grieve

"My eyes have grown dim from grief, and my whole body has become but a shadow."

JOB 17:7

Mom

"I have cancer," my mom calmly confessed as I leaned on the scratchy yellow couch behind me. As a child, I was old enough to know there was a problem, yet not mature enough to understand the nature of it. Tears were absent from her face, but children are skilled in sensing, and I knew something was wrong. I felt conflicted as she nonchalantly admitted she was sick and then went on with her housework. Grief, a "deep and poignant distress caused by or as if by bereavement,"[1] was what I felt; however, having no concept of grief, its intrusion was unsettling. In the days following my mom's life-shattering news, I got glimpses of grief, yet my parents' lack of emotional expression regarding her diagnosis translated to my young mind that pretending to be happy was just what you do. My inner pain was not validated by seeing their pain expressed. I suspect this led my eight-year-old mind to form the belief that my pain was wrong.

Not long after, I remember sneaking upstairs where my mom cradled my younger sister while surely contemplating what felt like a death sentence. The darkened loft in our apartment mimicked the dark sadness I felt clueless in communicating. As my eyes adjusted to the pitch-black room, I understood the movement of her body to be silent sobs. As an adult, and a mother myself, I now see the grief that must have flooded her like a tsunami. While she didn't tell me, I assume she was grieving the loss of what her life would be, the physical changes that were on the horizon, and possibly even death itself. I compassionately accept she did the best she knew how, but I also wonder if she thought by hiding her grief, she was being a loving shield for me.

What if I had been taught about grief by a mother who cried next to me rather than hidden from me? What if, instead of being my shield, this had been the hopeful, yet sorrowful way I learned to say, "But you, Lord, are a shield around me, my glory, and the one who lifts up my head" (Ps. 3:3)? I can only speculate, but I do think about these things as I try to raise my own children in an emotionally healthy way, grieving my lack of emotional health in childhood, yet compassionately respecting my mother who loved me the best she knew how.

In my teenage years, my mom's agonizing wails, reminiscent of a horror movie soundtrack, traveled to my basement bedroom through the air vents. She may have been lamenting her lot in life to the Lord, for the word *lament* in Hebrew means to wail, but I don't know for sure. What I do know is that my mom was in pain, most likely physical and definitely emotional pain. Parental concealment of emotional expression translates any wail of pain as something to be withheld from others. And withhold I did.

My learned behavior regarding pain was validated in the ballet studio. I was enrolled in ballet when I was three years old after weeks of twirling throughout our home wearing my favorite white petticoat. I not only loved ballet, but became known for it. I spent summers training with renowned companies such as American Ballet Theatre, Juilliard, and the Boston Ballet. But here's the problem with ballet: You are trained to give off the appearance of effortless beauty. Bloody toes and aching muscles were covered by satin pointe shoes and exquisite tutus. I was trained to gracefully dance with a pleasant expression on my face, completely withholding anything I felt so as not to ruin the experience of those I was performing for. Ballet is really just a creative form of people-pleasing. My whimsical movement on stage during lightning-speed footwork would transform into dry heaving in the wings at times. What a picture of masking pain in public while having grief-stricken panic attacks behind closed doors. I loved ballet, but it came at a cost. Ballet embodied cognitive dissonance, and the hours spent perfecting my art in the dance studio further hindered me in embracing my humanity.

Eventually, I believe my mom knew her end was approaching. Grief expert David Kessler wrote of Elisabeth Kübler-Ross, MD, "the mother of a movement that began to make grief a real conversation,"[2] that Elisabeth always said, "Listen to the dying. They will tell you everything you need to know about when they are dying. And it is easy to miss."[3] And I almost did. I was packing for my upcoming trip to Boston, where I would be dancing for six weeks after my freshman year at the University of Oklahoma. My mom uncharacteristically walked into my room and sat on my bed. Through long overdue tears, she abruptly said to me, "I'll never meet my grandchildren." Her heartbreaking disclosure validated what Elisabeth believed to be true. This was my dear mother finally showing me her grief. Being grief-illiterate, though, I pushed my pain away internally with unfortunate ease. I was only given a week in Boston before my final conversation with her over the phone brought news that there was nothing else the doctor could do.

She was given three months to live.

With her being sick most of my childhood, you'd assume I knew cancer would claim her life. Her concealed battle, though, meant news of her imminent death sent shockwaves through my heart. Her phone call was my unwelcomed introduction to anticipatory grief. My life multiplied much like the cancer cells killing her. I was operating in two worlds; one that still felt relatively normal, because life with her in it is all I knew, yet there was another world where I would have no mother, and I was trying to come to terms with what living in this strange land would mean. Generally, grief is thought of as a focus on what has been lost, however anticipatory grief maintains its focus on the loss ahead. It's within this tension that lament, a crying out to God in the midst of pain and confusion, attaches your heart in honesty and hope to Him, trusting His help will come. Today my faith-filled protest, while anticipating loss, would sound something like:

> "How long, Lord, is this cancer going to ravage her body? Why haven't you healed her yet? You would get the glory if you would. Are you really going to take away my mom? Help me, for I can't live without her. But I will trust in you, for you are faithful and I believe you will help me."

However, having no personal relationship with Him at the time, not only was the idea of honestly telling God how I felt ludicrous to me, but the word *lament* was simply not in my vocabulary. She died in the days following my arrival home, and while she was wide-awake in heaven, I metaphorically felt wide-awake in hell.

Grief was inescapable, and felt as though it really would kill me. Despite her drawn out illness, I didn't foresee her dying. "At an early age we momentarily anticipate that we can lose our parents. In our minds the thought is there, but denial helps us by telling us that it will happen to someone else's parents."[4] Days before her death, I was told she would die, but then I kind of didn't think she would. And then she did. I would never be the same. My mind was consumed by a concoction of thoughts—reminiscing over the beautiful days as her daughter, contemplating what I wish she had done differently, reliving the horrifying last moments of her life, and then also my terrifying future without a mom. The words of C. S. Lewis, in his beloved book *A Grief Observed*, feel as though they were written about me: "I not only live each endless day in grief, but live each day thinking about living each day in grief."[5]

She died in June.

We buried her in July.

I was back in college come August, pretending nothing had happened.

Dad

I stood stoically as loved ones offered me their condolences in the foyer of the mortuary following my father's funeral. I was an adult, as it had been a handful of years since we buried my mom, but even in my twenties, I felt the soul loneliness of orphanhood. The funeral attendees' warm tears were a tangible expression of the swelling sorrow that I felt trained to hide. My secret grief with my mom was the dress rehearsal for the performance of my life in concealing traumatic grief over my dad. No matter what was happening inside, my outward expression mimicked that of a ballerina—graceful and unscathed by pain. It was as though my emotions had been disconnected at best, but more accurately, locked away in a coffin, buried six feet below me. I didn't know how to articulate it, but I knew intuitively that appearing immune to grief, while burying my last remaining parent after his death by suicide, was weird.

Grieving my dad was confusing. He was my dad; I loved him and longed for him. Yet my lifelong yearning for the affection and attention I failed to receive from him left me bewildered at my sadness. I suppose I was also grieving what I never had, and while I can compassionately see that my dad gave me all he was capable of giving, I still wish it had been different. I grieve that it wasn't. What I now see with clarity was hidden in a tangled-up mess that I was able to ignore for a season. However, I've learned the hard way that grief ignored is a poison of sorts. Decades passed before I would begin to unpack that particular moment in the foyer, but that moment of discord in my soul would later catapult me into a journey characterized by hopeful sorrow. My sorrow has been held fast by hope as I've learned to understand grief, recognize complications within it, cry out to God in the midst of it, and walk in a state of loss adjustment.

Everyone Grieves

Secured by the original sin in Eden, grief is a tie that binds humanity together. It does not discriminate and is the natural response to losing what we know and love. Although the terms *grief* and *grieving* may be used interchangeably at times, they aren't quite the same. Grief is the emotion felt following loss, and while it may come in waves of varying strength, it lasts a lifetime. Grief feels shackled to you with no keys in sight; it's a shadow you cannot escape, a choke hold that won't let go.

Now raising my mom's grandkids she never got to see, I still feel grief when they do something I know she would have loved. In a world ready for you to move on from your grief, you may feel shame for lingering sorrow. Shame over grief, though, leads to concealing and complicating it. The truth is, we eventually adapt and learn to live with loss, but we never stop feeling some degree of anguish. Even years after loss has occurred, and your life has morphed into something meaningful again, there will be moments where the most minute reminder floods you with sadness. You keep going with a smile on your face; however, it's imperative that we normalize ongoing grief as the universal human experience.

While grief, though eventually tempered, becomes your lifelong companion in the wake of loss, grieving is a process. It has a trajectory. It's a journey that may include some or all of the well-known five stages of grief: denial, anger, bargaining, depression, and acceptance. The journey, though, will look different for each of us because grief is an individualized experience. The stages of grief have evolved since they were first introduced to the world and have been misunderstood at the same time. "They were never meant to help tuck messy emotions into neat packages. They are responses to loss that many people experience, but there is not a typical response to loss, as there is no typical loss. Our grief is as individual as our lives."[6] While not a neat road map with linear stops along the way, learning of these stages is helpful and hopeful in that they provide us with a framework for learning how to live after loss and for grasping grief's unpredictable terrain. You may skip around or alternate between various stages, or not experience certain stages altogether. Rather than a prescription for how to grieve, they should be viewed as a way to describe what grief may look like.

In considering various stages of grief, I suppose I was in denial during that disconnected moment in the foyer, for the initial response to overwhelming loss is often paralysis from shock or emotions running numb. "The denial is still not *denial of the actual death*, even though someone may be saying, 'I can't believe he's dead.' The person is actually saying that, at first, because it is too much for his or her psyche."[7] Perhaps denial was protecting me from an onslaught of emotion that was too much in the aftermath of my dad's suicide, but it wasn't long before things took a turn for the worse. Having lost one parent by natural causes and the other by choice taught me that grief can come in various shades, causing one to veer off the path of what is considered healthy grieving onto a more complicated one. I had veered. I was lost in a sea of complication, and it nearly cost me my life.

It's Complicated

Being a suicide survivor was never in my plans, and it can be confusing how the Lord could allow it to be. Unfortunately, I am not the only one who's been forced to join the dreaded group of those left behind, and sadly, I won't be the last. While suicide is preventable, it remains a leading cause of death in the United States, meaning each one of you reading this has been affected by suicide in one way or another. Grieving suicide is horrible and may involve feelings such as anger, betrayal, and shame, just to name a few.

The perceived abandonment tied to the intentionality of my dad's death pushed me into disorienting, complicated grief, also known as prolonged grief. While experts still seek clarity on prolonged grief, and if it is best to be labeled a disorder, in 2022 prolonged grief disorder was added to the *Diagnostic and Statistical Manual of Mental Disorders* (DSM-5-TR), a medical reference book used by doctors as a guide to help diagnose mental disorders. The entry states: "Prolonged grief disorder represents a prolonged maladaptive grief reaction that can be diagnosed only after at least 12 months (6 months in children and adolescents) have elapsed since the death of someone with whom the bereaved had a close relationship. Although in general this time frame reliably discriminates normal grief from grief that continues to be severe and impairing, the duration of adaptive grief may vary individually and cross-culturally."[8] This struggle may include a deep yearning for your loved one as well as a preoccupation with thinking of them. Other symptoms may include disbelief regarding the death; avoiding reminders of your loved one; excruciating, emotional pain; difficulty continuing or reengaging in relationships with others; and even struggling to plan the future. Complicated grief is savage. It's debilitating.

Suicide bereavement, along with grieving other types of traumatic deaths that are sudden, unexpected, and possibly violent, often leads to complicated grief, and it may include elements such as shock, bewilderment, and even a change in fundamental beliefs. "Those who have been bereaved by suicide may have symptoms of post-traumatic stress. If the person witnessed the death or found the body, they may suffer flashbacks or nightmares. This can also happen even if the person did not see them, but cannot stop imagining what happened—and imagination may be worse than reality."[9]

It is in these moments that turning to God in your grief, confusion, and questions through lament is essential to holding onto faith, even when circumstances are unbearable and unbelievable. Lament gives you permission to wrestle with that which is hard to wrap your mind around while still holding onto God's promises as if your life depends on it. And your life very well may depend on it. Initially, the signs and symptoms of normal grief and complicated grief may appear the same; however, over time, those of complicated grief linger and worsen whereas in normal grief, they fade.

Complicated grief is like being stuck in quicksand with no way out; the heightened state of mourning prevents healing. Processing through complicated grief may require the help of a trained professional, especially if there are thoughts of suicide involved. And while the exact causes of complicated grief remain unknown, it is believed that it may involve everything from your environment all the way to the chemical makeup of your body. For me, I believe my tightly clutched childhood conviction that revealing grief brought shame, so it was to be hidden, certainly played a part in my experience with complicated grief. I also did not know there was a hopeful way to cry out to God in the midst of persisting sadness over a complicated relationship with the loved one I lost. My dad's death happened after I accepted Jesus. I understood God to be sovereign and I did believe He loved me. I had faith that Jesus freed me from sin's grip, and I prayed. However, there was a richness lacking in my relationship with God, for not only did I fail to voice the complicated mess of thoughts that held my mind captive, but I thought telling God my true feelings was wrong. Essentially, I was still performing. I performed for my parents, I performed for audiences, and now I was performing for God. But God doesn't want our performance, He wants our hearts, complicated emotions and all.

In my story, complicated grief did not stand alone as the only mental health struggle. Not always, but complicated grief can most certainly coexist alongside depression and post-traumatic stress disorder (PTSD), as was the case for me. Although it would be nearly two decades following my dad's suicide before a mental breakdown and hospitalization would ensure I finally received the help I needed, I believe my struggles of major depressive disorder and PTSD had been prevalent for years, only further complicating the grieving process. The DSM-5-TR continues its entry, begun earlier: "The course of prolonged grief disorder may be complicated by comorbid posttraumatic stress disorder, which is more common in situations of bereavement following the violent death of a loved one (e.g., murder, suicide) when grief for the bereaved may be accompanied by personal life threat and/or witnessing of violent and potentially gruesome death."[10] Compared to those grieving nonviolent losses, there appears to be an association of prolonged grief disorder symptoms and suicidal ideation. Isolation, stigma, a lost sense of belonging, emotional distress, and avoiding reminders of the loss all carry a higher incidence of unhealthy behavior that is suicidal. My desperation to understand my dad's death collided with confusion as to why I cared so much about the man who abandoned me. This unhealthy obsession with all that had conspired invited suicidal ideation to the party.

Stuck in a Loop

As days melted into weeks and then years, my thoughts remained consumed by my dad's life, my experience as his daughter, and his traumatic death. Every detail surrounding his suicide played like a well-worn VHS tape from my childhood. My mind's eye would watch the horror of his death unfold, rewind, and repeat. While outwardly engaged in life, inwardly I withdrew deeper into continuous rehearsal of every detail. I would think on the moment I learned of his death through his written goodbye with ever-growing frequency and intensity. I imagined where he sat while he composed his final words, and I wondered if he ever considered his children as he penned those goodbyes. I longed for answers where there was no hope of receiving them, and I desperately wondered where God was. I felt rejected by my dad and God alike. You hear of miraculous intervention in suicide stories, but not in my dad's. I wanted to boldly ask God why. *Why didn't you stop him? Why didn't his method fail? Why would you not give him another chance?* I did not yet have a concept of lament, so those questions remained stuck in this unhealthy loop, this process we call rumination.

Unhealthy loops of rumination are antithetical to Paul's instruction to "take every thought captive" (2 Cor. 10:5), but rumination is common in those experiencing complicated grief, Christian and non-Christian alike. Rumination was my attempt to make sense of a nonsensical death, and my attempt at preventing the experience of such a loss again. Continually thinking on my dad's death, and imagining his final moments, fueled worry within me. What if I lose someone else like this? What if I follow in his footsteps? Although connected, worry and rumination differ in that rumination focuses on past negative events, and worry looks forward on the uncertainty of the future and possible negative outcomes. I was grief-stricken, but outwardly, I was holding it together. This grief was complicated and prolonged, lasting more than two decades. There was no anger, no bargaining, no acceptance, only depression. And deep, life-threatening depression at that.

For me, and maybe for you too, holding back from outwardly grieving out of self-preservation also meant holding it back from God. Turning inward and ruminating over my past distracted me from turning to the Father and releasing my pain. Worrying over my future distracted me from turning to the Father, knowing it was all in His loving hands. Trauma kept me in fight-or-flight and my suicidal ideation lied, telling me life would never have meaning.

Although finally receiving professional help changed the course of my life, it was abiding in Christ and experiencing a flourishing relationship with Him that brought me back to life. Connecting to Him as my life source is what transformed grief from a death sentence into a sorrowful teacher that unlocked the beauty of hope like nothing else has.

So, what is the proper way to grieve, not as the world grieves, but with hope (1 Thess. 4:13) even in persisting sorrow? Is there actually a way for meaningless expressions of agony to be transformed into faith-filled cries to God who can comfort and act on our behalf? While the worldwide church is made up of believers within their cultural norms across the globe, one similarity remains regardless of earthly citizenship. This is where we usher lament fully into our conversation. Lament is not just something to think about in the grieving process, it's the primary way a follower of Christ should grieve. It's through lament that we experience the mystery of grief coexisting with a mind captivated by Christ rather than crushing circumstances. It's how we wrestle with the pain that seems incomprehensible, and it's the grace of God given to us so that we may grieve in a healthy and attached way to Him.

Reflection Questions

1. When were you first introduced to grief in your life?

2. Are you currently grieving a loss?

3. Do you feel that you have veered off the path of healthy grief into complicated grief?

CHAPTER 2

What Is Lament?

*"Listen to my words, LORD, consider my lament.
Hear my cry for help, my King and my God, for to you I pray."*

PSALM 5:1–2 NIV

Lament is defined as "a passionate expression of grief or sorrow,"[1] and if this demonstrative form of prayer were an animal, it would not be domesticated. It's not aimlessly crying over sorrow or making peace with despair, as despair is devoid of hope while lament demands it. Longing to see purpose produced from pain, lament believes God can bring good from excruciating evil meant to harm. Through brazen, goal-oriented language that implores God to act, lament fights the apathy of depression and unease of anxiety through hope and action. When loss pushes you to plumb the depths of grief, lament fights the urge to turn away from God in despondency by turning toward Him in desperation.

Feeling despondent and yielding to despondency are different. Yielding to despondency is to make friends with it, essentially declaring your hope dead rather than living. We, brothers and sisters, don't make peace with despondency, we make war. We stand strengthened by the Lord and engage in the good fight of faith by putting on the full armor of God (Eph. 6:11). Along with that, we "Pray at all times in the Spirit with every prayer and request, and stay alert with all perseverance and intercession for all the saints" (v. 18). Lament is the prayer language of perseverance in the midst of spiritual warfare as it calls on the God who fights for you to act on your behalf. Choosing despondency over declaring war is rooted in unbelief, because unbelief accepts defeat. Giving up in the fight for your faith is to allow sin to have dominion over you rather than choose to be governed by God's grace. And God's grace is seen in our ability to turn to Him in belief, often seen by the word *but*.

> My flesh and my heart may fail,
> *but* God is the strength of my heart,
> my portion forever.
> (Ps. 73:26, emphasis mine)

Your health, your heart, and every circumstance in your life may fail, but your Father in heaven will not. Emotional health and maturity are not found in the absence of struggle, but through faith in the struggle. This very act of turning, which the use of *but* indicates, is the truest form of faith as that which is based on what we believe rather than what we see and feel. And not just turning to look at God, but turning to *really* see Him; to address Him in belief that He, in fact, does hear our prayers. *But* represents the resolve necessary to trust God even if your circumstances appear to oppose His loving-kindness. Shadrach, Meshach, and Abednego lived with the resolve *but* represents. When King Nebuchadnezzar threatened to throw them in the fiery furnace for not bowing down to a gold statue, they replied: "If the God we serve exists, then he can rescue us from the furnace of blazing fire, and he can rescue us from the power of you, the king. *But* even if he does not rescue us, we want you as king to know that we will not serve your gods or worship the gold statue you set up" (Dan. 3:17–18, emphasis mine).

Because "Faith is confidence in what we hope for and assurance about what we do not see" (Heb. 11:1 NIV), admitting that your flesh and heart may fail highlights the miracle of your faith. Through faith in Christ, we have a settled confidence that is not wishful thinking born of imagination or even the ideal circumstances. Faith is being persuaded that the promises of God, regardless of how feasible they appear, will transpire because God is eternal, good, sovereign, trustworthy, wise, and all-powerful, and because we look to Scripture as our absolute truth in understanding our Lord. Faith calls us to do what may appear foolish to the world, but God made the deliberate choice to use the foolish things of the world to shame those that view themselves wise. Human nature would view Abraham's near-sacrifice of his beloved son, Isaac, to be foolishness; however, Abraham's faith looked past his knife to the God he was convinced could raise Isaac from the dead. Abraham chose to obey God regardless of how foolish it may have seemed; He chose to believe. Through Abraham's faith, he was counted righteous by the Lord (Gen. 15:6). Lamenting pain to the God whose providence allowed it may seem foolish to some, but what do they know of God's miraculous mercy that, in reality, shines with absolute love?

When pain paints God as hateful, we can curse God and die like Job's wife suggested, or we can turn to God in hopeful sorrow. One option answers Satan's call, while the other takes the posture of grief and worship, declaring: "Should we accept only good from God and not adversity?" (Job 2:10). Job's humble sentiment does not abolish his sorrow, but rather shows that even in sorrow, faith is possible. Job illustrates that we can accept adversity from God and still cry to Him over it. Those who have invalidated your pain, by hushing your vocalization of confusion in the name of faith, don't understand how worshipful weeping binds a bleeding heart to the Father. God doesn't invalidate pain. I believe He does the exact opposite. The inclusion of lament in the Bible acts as a divine invitation for us to join those in Scripture who have wrestled with the hard things of this world. Lament doesn't suppress hurt, but offers an outlet to express it. Lament is the unique language belonging to the children of God. It is not simply crying, but rather praying the sorrow you're convinced will kill you back to God with the purpose of renewing hope in Him.

Lament Is Countercultural

Social media bombards us with the allusion of perfection. Lament is countercultural in that it challenges the social norm of curating, filtering, and presenting the perfect life for all to see. It's revolutionary. It's authentic. And while it falls under Ecclesiastes' claim that "there is nothing new under the sun" (Eccles. 1:9), the modern church has somehow lost touch with this ancient song of sorrow in need of resurrection. In a day of deconstructing faith and desperation for authenticity, our world is ripe for lament. The mental health crisis, along with its soaring number of suicides, speaks to the shift that must happen within the church. We are told at church to look on the bright side, silencing us from bemoaning loss and isolating us within our individual stories of sadness, but how can this be God's way? Under the guise of optimism, or dare I say joy, this disconnected, tone-deaf way of life is reflected through shallow, cheerful prayers. Lament is for those brave and humble enough to forsake prayers of performance for jarring prayers of relationship, for it's through the shocking language of lament that grief is miraculously juxtaposed by hope, and intimacy with God is forged.

The loss of lament within the church has not helped us grow closer to each other. In fact, it has done the opposite. This travesty nurtures the Enemy's goal of separated saints losing hope in their sorrow, shrinking away from the very pews they once sat. Therefore, practicing lament both individually and communally becomes a weapon of hope as we fight for faith together. Consider how unsettling it would be to hear someone lament during the opening prayer of Sunday's service using this unfiltered language:

> Why is light given to one burdened with grief,
> and life to those whose existence is bitter,
> who wait for death, but it does not come,
> and search for it more than for hidden treasure,
> who are filled with much joy
> and are glad when they reach the grave?
> (Job 3:20–22)

An awkward silence would ensue, only interrupted by humor to deflect the depressed words as if they were a disease to be caught by those in their Sunday best. But how many of us resonate with Job's vulnerable vocabulary? It's ironic that we'd label the source of those words to be irreverent and lacking in faith when, in reality, he was a "man of perfect integrity, who fears God and turns away from evil" (Job 1:8). I know the loneliness of carrying pain into the sanctuary and feeling like no one else is hurting like me. Mouthing happy praise songs in the wake of loss feels hollow and incongruent. A song full of hallelujahs may appear triumphant—and it is—however, I would argue that guttural groans are just as victorious when they are directed toward the God of hope who, even in your sorrow, can "fill you with all joy and peace as you believe so that you may overflow with hope by the power of the Holy Spirit" (Rom. 15:13).

The word *lament* has all but been erased from the vocabulary of the faith community, including worship songs and funeral services. While death opens the door to eternal joy for the Christian, death is still our enemy. And it is right to express anger at its existence, even at the same memorial service deemed a celebration of life. When Lazarus died, Mary ran to Jesus and said, "Lord, if you had been here, my brother wouldn't have died!" (John 11:32). As Jesus looked at her, He "was deeply moved in his spirit and troubled" (v. 33).

Jesus grieved over the death of Lazarus, as well as the grief his loved ones were experiencing. Jesus displayed emotional maturity through the concoction of emotion he expressed. Our Man of Sorrows felt sadness over loss, anger over the presence of death, and coexisting awe over death being rendered powerless through His upcoming death and resurrection. Jesus feeling simultaneous joy and sorrow, hope and grief, and anger and awe offers us a template to do the same.

When your grief on earth collides with your hope of heaven, it can feel complicated. You know one day your sorrow will end when God wipes away your last tear (Rev. 21:4), yet that day is not today. The Christian life is one great paradox. As mysterious as God is, we are invited to know Him. He is sovereign and yet allows us to choose salvation. He is loving and has wrath. He is merciful and just, and we live by dying. Being embodied by grief and hope, lament is the language of paradox. We know that Jesus defeated death through His resurrection, yet we live in the tension between grief and glory where people still die. From an eternal perspective, we declare: "Death has been swallowed up in victory. Where, death, is your victory? Where, death, is your sting?" (1 Cor. 15:54b–55), but while still bound on this earth, feel the heartbreaking enemy to be the bane of our existence. Yes, death is a gateway into joy everlasting, but on earth our joy is—and will always be—polluted by death and the loss it represents. Therefore, we lament.

As I am writing this chapter, I am being challenged to put my words into practice. I just spent the weekend teaching the Bible at a women's event, with an emphasis on mental health. I felt the Spirit guide me in specifically speaking on suicide. Women flooded me afterward with stories of loss. Mothers, children, husbands, siblings, best friends, and even believers, all dead at their own hand. I offered my listening ear and pointed them to Christ, but that did not bring back their loved ones. It did not erase flashbacks of finding bodies or rewire their traumatized brains. Yes, nothing is impossible for God, but we live in a broken world where we must endure pain. This is where lament offers the outlet to tell God exactly how unbearable life feels, but from the foundation of faith that He is in control and will someday make all things new. More than a cathartic release, lament implores God to arise and act. In the wake of loss, maybe God is not bringing your loved one back, but He can certainly act by filling you with hope, providing for your needs, and sustaining you with His grace. And so I sit here, lamenting my pain to God. Sorrow over their losses, but also sorrow over mine triggered by theirs. Sorrow mixed with anger at the Enemy's apparent victory; yet hope, knowing Jesus has already won. "You know that the testing of your faith produces endurance" (James 1:3), and lament is the language of endurance as we turn toward God in the furnace of affliction where that very faith is being tested.

You can both declare the grave has no hold on you and yet grieve over those in a grave. You can wrestle with why God has allowed abuse and still choose to tell Him, "You are good and do good" (Ps. 119:68 ESV). And miraculously, prayers of lament and joyful praise can flow from the same vessel, as David so poignantly demonstrates throughout the Psalter. Perhaps David was unstable in his seemingly changing moods, or maybe he just understood how praise and pain can reside in the same person.

David wasn't the only one who lamented in Scripture. Many of our heroes of the faith lamented, such as Job, Naomi, Habakkuk, Moses, Hannah, and Jeremiah, and we are given the entire book of Lamentations which weeps over Jerusalem's destruction. Expressions of grief and lament weren't always a quiet matter either. Various places in Scripture show that sometimes professional mourners were hired to lament at funerals by wailing, weeping, and creating quite a commotion to reflect the grief of death. Jesus also lamented, as seen in the last hours of His life and when He quoted Psalm 22 while hanging on the cross. If lament is so prevalent in the Bible, it's time that we explore this lost language of hope on its pages.

The Psalter

The beloved Psalter, comprised of 150 poems, was essentially the song book for Israel in their gathered worship. Within the pages of Psalms, you will find a variety of themes, but over a third of the psalms fall under the category of lament. These songs cover an extensive range of emotions, many of which were written from the stories of real people that are still relevant today. Because of their relatability and encouragement, the Psalms may be the most loved and read book in the entire Bible, offering vocabulary to express the variety of emotions unique to the human experience. "At the same time, the psalms do not simply *express* emotions: when sung in faith, they actually *shape* the emotions of the godly. The emotions are therefore not a problem to be solved but are part of the raw material of now-fallen humanity that can be shaped to good and noble ends."[2] When grief seemingly steals your words, psalms of lament provide not only an outline, but the expressive dialect to adopt as your own.

Prayer

Prayer has a direct aim at God, the recipient of your confession, petition, supplication, intercession, praise, and thanksgiving. While there are other words used for prayer in the Bible, one that dominates the space is *proseuchomai*, a word for prayer in Greek, the original language of the New Testament. The prefixed preposition *pros* carries the idea of toward facing. It's a directness in prayer, with the idea of talking face-to-face with God. *Proseuchomai* was used in classical Greek as a term for evoking a deity; however, we see this term transformed in the New Testament as a word that describes genuine conversation with God. *Euchomai* simply means to pray, but when you add *pros* to it to form the word *proseuchomai*, you see the idea of turning toward and moving close to God in prayer.

Another word used for prayer in the New Testament is *deesis*, which refers to requests that are urgent, arising from one's desperate need. With *deesis*, we see a turn toward God followed by a plea made from a realization that God is the one who can supply what you are lacking. Looking into verses that use *deesis* illustrates the meaning of this word. In Scripture, we see an eighty-four-year-old widow who fasted and prayed day and night in the temple (Luke 2:36–37 ESV). We see an angel tell Zechariah that his prayer had been heard and that his wife, Elizabeth, would have a child (Luke 1:13). Paul prays for the salvation of his fellow Jews (Rom. 10:1) and uses this word when he encourages the Philippians to forsake anxiety and tells them to make their requests known to God through prayer (Phil. 4:6). Each situation involved a need expressed to the Father. Most notably, we see *deesis* in regard to Jesus, who "During his earthly life, he offered prayers [deesis] and appeals with loud cries and tears to the one who was able to save him from death, and he was heard because of his reverence. Although he was the Son, he learned obedience from what he suffered" (Heb. 5:7–8). While Jesus' gut-wrenching prayer in the garden of Gethsemane is one of His most well-known laments, the phrase *during his earthly life* suggests that Jesus' earthly prayers were consistently heartfelt and tearful, rather than few and far between. It's remarkable that the God of the universe invites us to turn to Him and move close as we share every need, every want, every fear, every grief, and every deep, dark secret with Him. With a deeper understanding of prayer in general, let's further investigate lament.

Turning in Faith

When lamenting our pain, the first step is to turn toward God. Even though the language within the lament may be expressive, or even irrational, the fact that your words are directed to the Lord indicates that you believe He is there to hear them. Here are some examples:

> Out of the depths I call to you, Lord!
> Lord, listen to my voice;
> let your ears be attentive
> to my cry for help.
> (Ps. 130:1–2)

> Lord, why do you stand so far away?
> Why do you hide in times of trouble?
> (Ps. 10:1)

Lament is the language of God's children who understand their need for help, and so they draw near to God's throne of grace and ask for it. Turning to God affirms your dependance on Him, as it takes humility to realize you cannot fix your situation, ease your grief, or unlock your shackles on your own. The initial turning toward God may not necessarily remove your sorrow, but it is a declaration that there is still hope within it.

Complaint

The next element is complaint, but because we are taught not to complain, you may be wondering how this is permissible. Israel's response to the Lord's miraculous deliverance from Egypt was not lifting up God in praise and worship, but rather grumbling, which did not please the Lord. "The Lord spoke to Moses and to Aaron, saying, 'How long shall this wicked congregation grumble against me? I have heard the grumblings of the people of Israel, which they grumble against me'" (Num. 14:26–27 ESV). There is a difference between the complaint seen in lament and the complaints of the Israelites. The Israelites were complaining in a way that attacked the character of God, whereas David complained that his difficulty felt incongruent with God's character. Worldly complaint typically involves anger at God, which sinfully arises from the one who wrongly believes God owes them something. Worldly complaint also misinterprets God's sovereign action as hateful and would never consider that perhaps the goodness of God does not fit into our human definition of good. Godly complaint, however, believes God's character to be good, rich in mercy, and abounding in steadfast love. This type of complaint is full of faith, as it rightly views God while simultaneously trying to reconcile difficult circumstances that appear opposed to His promises. When we know and believe God is good, yet our circumstances don't feel good, we can tell Him how confusing that is.

We live in a broken world full of bewildering pain. In God's deep compassion for us, He has given us examples of how to express our pain to Him like David, who prayed, "Hear me, my God, as I voice my complaint; protect my life from the threat of the enemy" (Ps. 64:1 NIV). The psalms of lament are a salve for the troubled saints on their way home to heaven. They give us permission to voice the anguish we are told to expect in this world from a place of belief. "For everyone who has been born of God overcomes the world. And this is the victory that has overcome the world—our faith" (1 John 5:4 ESV). Our perfect behavior, good circumstances, and our performative prayers that sound pleasing from a social media platform aren't what overcomes the world, it's our faith. In Psalm 13, an individual lament where David feels that he cannot endure any longer, we see complaint as he voices feeling forgotten and ignored by God:

> How long, LORD? Will you forget me forever?
> How long will you hide your face from me? (v. 1)

Scripture tells us that God will never abandon His children nor forget them. In Hebrews 13:5 God says, "I will never leave you or abandon you." In Isaiah 49:15, God tells us: "I will not forget you." We know God did not forget or forsake David, but David felt as if he had. "If psalms were theological treatises, they would affirm that God will not forget his people (cf. 9:12) and that the abandonment described here is only apparent. But a song, whose goal is to describe feelings, does not need the same level of precision and detachment as a treatise."[3] Even though David's feelings did not align with truth, they were real to David and worthy of acknowledgment. It was good and right for David to let himself feel this way and then take those feelings to God. It's through lament that those feelings find their way to faith. David's pain was excruciating for him in the deep pit of despair, but from his sorrow birthed a hopeful lament that has become one of the greatest encouragements to the church.

Now, let's look at some examples of godly complaint:

> My God, my God, why have you forsaken me?
> Why are you so far from saving me, from the
>   words of my groaning?
> O my God, I cry by day, but you do not answer,
>   and by night, but I find no rest.
> (Ps. 22:1–2 ESV)

> LORD, why do you stand so far away?
> Why do you hide in times of trouble? (Ps. 10:1)

Request

While lament involves articulating your suffering to God, it also asks God to intervene. To lament is to be aware of your human limitations in fixing or alleviating whatever need you have. Lament is a choice, and while that may sound daunting to the one struggling to find motivation within their depression, or a calm frame of mind in the midst of anxiety, lament fights feeling out of control by giving you agency. When we discover we have a voice in our suffering, and use that voice to express our need to God, we feel heard, which lends itself to hope.

In 1 Samuel 1, we are introduced to Hannah, a woman who was desperate to have a child and attributed her infertility to the Creator. In her grief, she would weep and not eat. "'Hannah, why are you crying?' her husband, Elkanah, would ask. 'Why won't you eat? Why are you troubled? Am I not better to you than ten sons?'" (v. 8). One day, she turned to God and cried out in prayer. The emotions inside her do not point to a lack of faith because we see those emotions point her to the Father. "She was deeply distressed and prayed to the LORD and wept bitterly" (v. 10 ESV). When Eli, a priest, approached Hannah, accusing her of being drunk because of her passionate lament, she described herself by saying, "'I am a woman with a broken heart. I haven't had any wine or beer; I've been pouring out my heart before the LORD. Don't think of me as a wicked woman; I've been praying from the depth of my anguish and resentment.' Eli responded, 'Go in peace, and may the God of Israel grant the request you've made of him.' 'May your servant find favor with you,' she replied. Then Hannah went on her way; she ate and no longer looked despondent" (vv. 15b–18). After Hannah prayed, yet before she saw the outcome, she was able to eat again and no longer looked despondent, because she hadn't yielded to it. Lamenting, for her, and for us too, turned her heart toward hope.

Hannah's prayer reminds me of my own heart-crushing situations, encouraging me to run to God, even when He has allowed my sorrow. Hannah knew God could not only ease her pain, but that He could reverse her pain by giving her a child. "After some time, Hannah conceived and gave birth to a son. She named him Samuel, because she said, 'I requested him from the Lord'" (v. 20).

The presence of distress does not equal a lack of faith or that someone has forsaken godliness. Even in her deep sadness, Hannah was a godly woman. "As we read the chapter, we can be sure that her heart was right with God. We cannot raise any question about the sincerity of her prayer, or the prevalence of it. We do not doubt for a moment the truthfulness of her holy joy, the confidence of her faith, or the strength of her consecration. She was one that feared God above many, an eminently gracious woman, and yet 'a woman of a sorrowful spirit.'"[4] Hannah's request is just one of many requests seen in the Bible. Here are others in various psalms of lament:

> Arise, O Lord! Confront him, subdue him!
>   Deliver my soul from the wicked by your sword.
> (Ps. 17:13 ESV)

> Rise up, Lord God! Lift up your hand.
> Do not forget the oppressed.
> (Ps. 10:12)

Choose to Trust

The final element of lament is a confession of trust in God. After we turn to God in faith, articulate our pain, complain, and make requests, we must actively choose to place our trust and hope in Him, even if the outcome to our prayer remains unknown. As post-resurrection people of God, our prayers of lament are anchored in our beliefs about God's character as described in Scripture. While the psalmists certainly displayed hope in their trust, we can know on a deeper level, through Jesus, that God will meet us in our sorrowful cries and walk with us through every shadowy valley of death. Here are some examples:

> But I will see your face in righteousness;
> when I awake, I will be satisfied with your presence.
> (Ps. 17:15)

> I will thank the LORD for his righteousness;
> I will sing about the name of the LORD Most High.
> (Ps. 7:17)

> But you heard the sound of my pleading
> when I cried to you for help.
> (Ps. 31:22b)

Now that we have walked through the typical steps of a lament, let's look at all of them put together in one place by looking at Psalm 13.

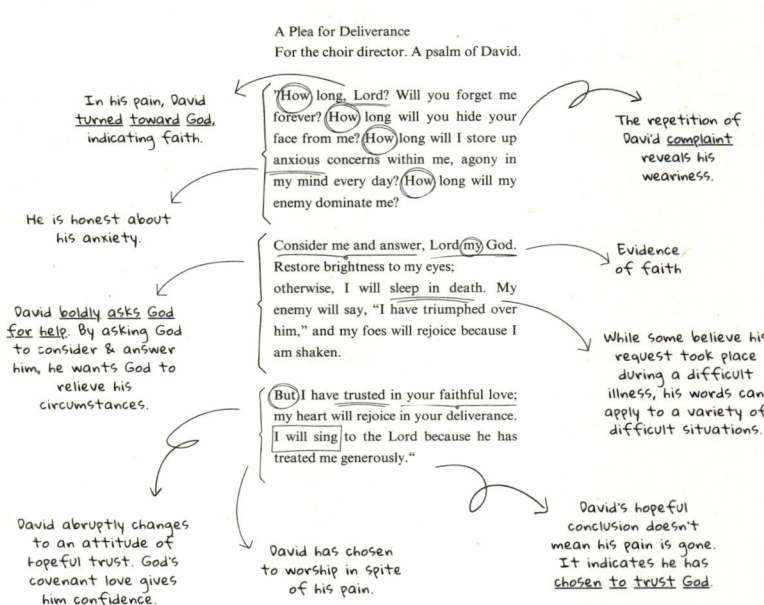

When Darkness Doesn't Lift

But what do we do when the idea of ending a lament in confident trust, or even joy, seems impossible? If this is you, allow me to gift you the dark words of Psalm 88, which are not to be misunderstood as faithless, for remember who these words were spoken to.

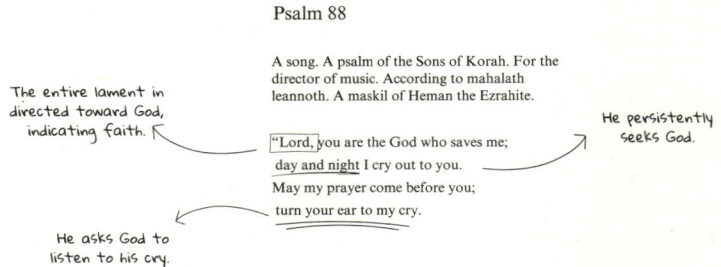

This individual lament resonates with those who know what it's like to be so overwhelmed with troubles that it feels like even loved ones stand far off. The specifics of the singer's plight may be vague, but the depth of his distress isn't. Psalm 88 gives assurance to those feeling overthrown by despair that faith is still possible in the midst of such emotional turmoil. "The psalm allows the singer to lay out these despairing feelings; it does not claim that such feelings correspond to reality. Indeed, anyone genuinely singing this to *the Lord*, however miserable he may feel, can be assured that he is still expressing true faith. And yet these despairing feelings produce genuine pain, whether or not they correspond to reality."[5] In a world full of whitewashed tombs, saying all the eloquent phrases in language laced with Christianese, how refreshing is it to see someone honestly admit to God that they feel as though they are among the dead? And remember, God brings dead things back to life.

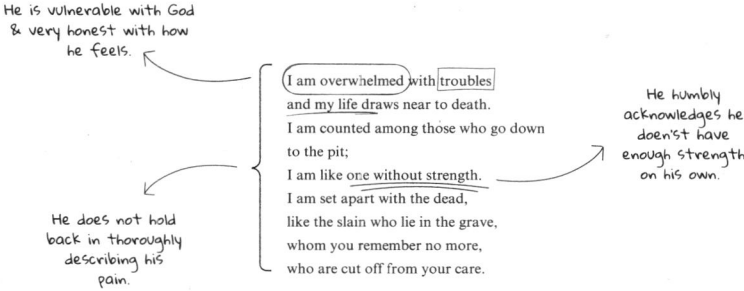

I suspect God would rather hear despairing words from a saint fighting for their faith over empty words from a Pharisee performing for fame. Unlike other laments, there is no explicit confession of confidence and hope in Psalm 88. If we take a closer look, though, we can see a glimmer of confidence in verses 6 and 7, as the song credits God with being the one to usher the troubles into his life, implying relief is found in the Lord as well:

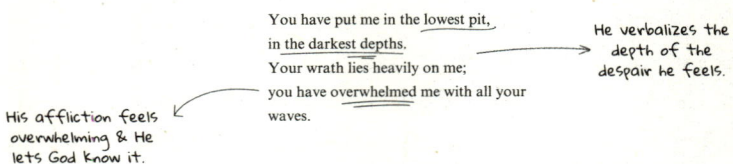

As the singer continues, we see the desperation he feels within the circumstances he feels trapped by. At the same time, the congregations singing these words are reminded to call upon the Lord repeatedly when they, too, feel alone and trapped.

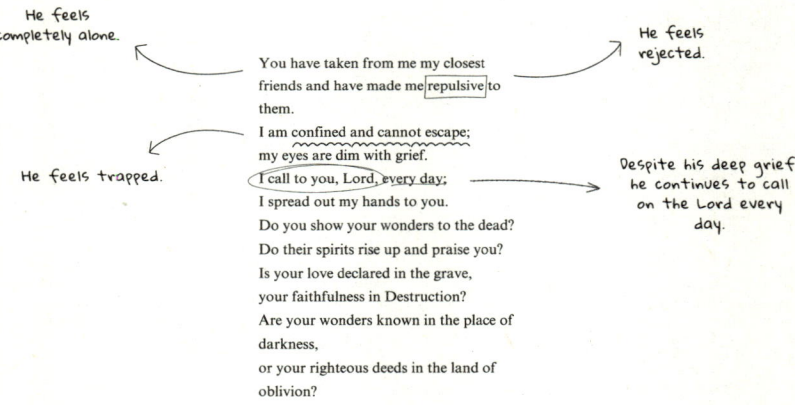

Alone and trapped. How many of us have felt that way when the darkness seems to settle over us with no sign of light breaking in? Feeling alone and trapped can contribute to suicidal tendencies, but within this psalm, we see that even when you feel this way, you can still call upon the Lord in faith. As Psalm 88 progresses, the singer continues to voice his despairing feelings, even articulating his perceived abandonment by God:

WHAT IS LAMENT?

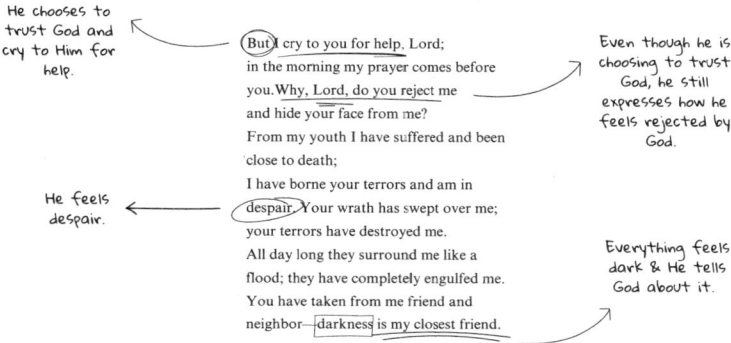

While God will never abandon you, you may find it comforting that the author of this sad psalm, which was sung by God's people, felt this way too. And God included this in the canon. Woven throughout this psalm are expressions of isolation. The psalmist feels as though those you would expect help and support from have shunned him, leaving darkness as his only friend.

Darkness, not light.

Is that the typical song you sing in your church?

Probably not, but isn't it comforting to those of us who have been in the pit?

While the ending is somber, it's not hopeless. Children of God know that there really is no other way to endure depression other than seeking the Lord in prayer, even if it feels like no one is listening. I can assure you, your laments do not fall on deaf ears, for your Shepherd sees you, hears you, and He is with you as you walk through the valley.

Reflection Questions

1. Is lament a new concept for you?

2. Were you raised being told it was okay to tell God how you really feel?

3. Why do you think lament is lacking in the church today?

Now it's your turn. Grab a journal and write your own lament. In appendix 1 you'll find words that may help you describe what you're feeling, and in appendix 2, you'll find a guide for response and prayer as you reflect on this chapter.

CHAPTER 3

Practicing Lament

I pray to you, O LORD, my rock. Do not turn a deaf ear to me. For if you are silent, I might as well give up and die. Listen to my prayer for mercy as I cry out to you for help . . .

PSALM 28:1–2a NLT

"Have a good day," I cheerfully said to my daughter as she grabbed her clarinet and hopped out of my car. Upon leaving her school, I merged onto the highway, when I saw something my mind could not compute. I saw a lifeless mass on the road, and while I could recognize it to be a person, the shock of what I was witnessing made me reason that it was anything but. Where was the car he must have flown out of and where were the first responders? As panic grew, my gut knew. There was no wrecked car because this wasn't a wreck. He had just died by suicide, and I was among the first on the scene.

The days following this public trauma were a whirlwind of emotion; namely, confusion and anger. Imagining his family receiving the news triggered the moment I received my dad's suicide note. And speaking of that, why, of all people, would God allow *me* to see such a horrific moment? That scene was seared on my mind that day, and although it has softened, so to speak, the scar remains. It didn't take long for my initial shock to be eclipsed by anger. And while my anger may have been misdirected, it was still within the confines of faith since I believed God heard my questions:

> *"Why did I see that, God? I have to drive by this spot every time I go speak at events about mental health. Why would you want to trigger me before I do Your work?"*

My inner peace felt assaulted by the Prince of Peace, and my response to this perceived attack was to fight back, for anger triggers us to do something. But there was really nothing I could do since I couldn't erase that memory. Over time, my distress tolerance increased, and through therapy, I learned how to cope with the flashbacks, but in that moment, my bandwidth was miniscule. I was taken aback by my anger, but was too ashamed to confront it. God felt aloof and I didn't know what to do with a God who refused to remain in the box I put Him in. This turned me away from Him. In *The Cry of the Soul* by Dr. Dan B. Allender and Dr. Tremper Longman II, we see that "Anger attempts to rectify God's passivity by empowering us to act instead of waiting vulnerably for God to do something. It is not only a protection against harm and an energizer for battle; it is a taunt against God for apparently refusing to act on our behalf."[1] I felt attacked by God and resonated with Job's use of warfare imagery that expressed how he felt God had charged at him:

> I was at ease, but he shattered me; he seized me by the scruff of the neck and smashed me to pieces. He set me up as his target; his archers surround me. He pierces my kidneys without mercy and pours my bile on the ground. He breaks through my defenses again and again; he charges at me like a warrior. I have sewn sackcloth over my skin; I have buried my strength in the dust. (Job 16:12–15)

Job's grief is likened to coarse cloth sewn to his skin. This graphic picture conjures up a visceral response in those of us who know what it's like to exist with acute and seemingly never-ending pain. The ancient practice of putting on sackcloth and ashes served as an outward token of the inner grief and desperation those who wore them experienced. I wasn't donning sackcloth, and there were no ashes to be found, but my grief was just as uncomfortable as that sackcloth must have felt back then. My view of God up until now had been burnt up, leaving ashes all around, with no hope of beauty emerging.

God not shielding me from seeing that scene felt like an attack on me personally, but also on my view of God. Both experientially and cognitively, I had come to believe God to be good (Ps. 119:68), trustworthy (Ps. 145:13), protecting (Ps. 46:2), faithful (1 Thess. 5:24), merciful (Ps. 86:5), and loving (1 John 3:1). I didn't know how to reconcile a God who appeared in opposition to those traits. God is our helper, but in that moment on the road, I questioned if He had really helped me.

I believed He had hurt me.

In Psalm 3, David expresses his confidence in God while he fled from his son Absalom (see 2 Sam. 15–16). David began by crying to God regarding the many foes that were attacking him. He lamented: "Many say about me, 'There is no help for him in God'" (v. 2). This infernal accusation against God stands as a divide in the path. Will David turn away in despair or toward God in faith? God had not prevented David from being attacked, but He did prove to be with him in the midst of it. In reading those taunting words from the masses, I realized who my real Enemy was. And it wasn't God. When my eyes took in that traumatic, public death, I assumed God was the one attacking me. In hindsight, I see that I equated the absence of suffering with being shielded, and listened to the Enemy, that there was no help for me in God. Like a child telling his dad about the bully at school, David took his painful experience of being attacked by his foes straight to God. David chose to see through eyes of faith as he responded to others claiming God would be of no help to him by declaring within his lament: "But you, LORD, are a shield around me, my glory, and the one who lifts up my head" (v. 3). There it is again. *But.*

David was no stranger to God as his shield and source of help, both in his own life, and in the stories of God's people passed down to him. God has always fought for His people. In the great story of the exodus, the Israelites found themselves in distress as the Egyptians pursued them. "Moses answered the people, 'Do not be afraid. Stand firm and you will see the deliverance the LORD will bring you today. The Egyptians you see today you will never see again. The LORD will fight for you; you need only to be still'" (Exod. 14:13–14 NIV). The Lord has, is, and will always fight for his people. David, like Moses, who "persevered as one who sees him who is invisible" (Heb. 11:27), relied on God to fight for him. We see this faithful help from God in Psalm 35:

> Contend, O LORD, with those who contend with me; fight against those who fight against me! Take hold of shield and buckler and rise for my help! Draw the spear and javelin against my pursuers! Say to my soul, "I am your salvation!" (vv. 1–3 ESV)

Psalm 35, an individual lament, may begin with a cry for help against those who pursue him, but it ends in hopeful expectation that he will rejoice over God's sure deliverance.

> Let those who delight in my righteousness shout for joy and be glad and say evermore, "Great is the LORD, who delights in the welfare of his servant!" Then my tongue shall tell of your righteousness and of your praise all the day long. (vv. 27–28 ESV)

There are times God shields us physically from suffering, but there are also times he shields us spiritually *within* the suffering. As

I realized the difference, my heart found solace in David's cries of pain in Psalm 28:

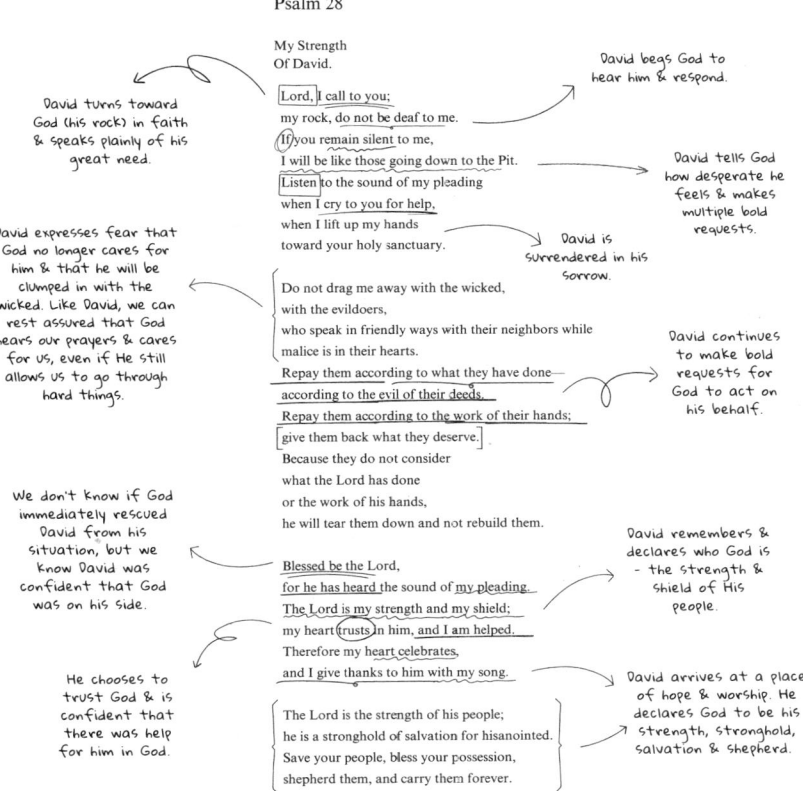

The same passion in the opening of David's prayer of lament was still present as he ended in praise. His hopeful sorrow not only tempered my sorrow with hope, but caused me to question my confidence in God as my shield. Scripture began realigning my perspective of God with truth, but I still could not see how God could bring good from me seeing that man's body. God had used my parents' deaths to teach me that He is my true Father. He had even used my dad's death of despair to spur me on to share with others that Jesus is life. But this? This seemed unnecessary and even a little cruel, if I'm being honest. My cry echoed that of Job:

> I cry to you for help and you do not answer me;
> I stand, and you only look at me.
> You have turned cruel to me;
> with the might of your hand you persecute me.
> (Job 30:20–21 ESV)

At first glance, Job's words seem unbiblical and lacking in faith. We must remember, though, that this honest lament came from the one deemed the most blameless and upright on earth during his lifetime by God (Job 1:8). Scripture's honesty invites us into those frustrating, overwhelming, and disappointing moments of the in-between where we can insert our own tragic stories. Job felt like every cry of his heart was met with a cold God who refused to act on his behalf. Can you relate? But God *was* acting on Job's behalf, even if His activity was actively withholding intervention until the timing was right. Job's story teaches us to trust God no matter what is happening. In his shortsightedness, Job could not see that his continued trust in God was putting Satan to shame. While Job writhed in pain, God was writing a story that we are still being encouraged by to this day. There was purpose in God allowing Job's affliction, and while we are able to see the redemption at the end of Job's story, it is no accident that God gave us a loving glimpse into those in-between, messy moments full of lament. Perhaps I am still waiting to see the full expression of goodness that will surely shine through my witnessing of that man on the road, but I can assure you, the way that public suicide has thrust me into the practice of lament has surely infused the sorrow with supernatural sweetness.

Now Lament It

After nine months of processing that public suicide with my counselor, as well as staying in Scripture in an effort to remember God's character, I left therapy one afternoon in distress and drove home. Therapy proved integral in processing the trauma, but also incomplete in my healing, as a wall remained between my heart and God. I beelined for my closet and slumped to the ground. I impulsively grabbed the nearest journal and scribbled line after line of the raw emotion that overwhelmed me. I applied no filter nor took any time to nurture the wordsmith nestled within me. My handwriting rebelled against my inner perfectionist, and my sentences were childlike and choppy. After filling up the page, I held my journal up and was taken aback by the darkness presented through my pen. Would anyone believe a Christian wrote those words? As I stared at that page, I felt the Lord ever so gently, but quite directly, say to my spirit, "Now lament it." It was like a lightning bolt.

Sitting in limbo between spiraling and surrendering, I remembered my therapist introducing me to a list of common, unhealthy thinking patterns that I quickly recognized throughout this journal entry. Cognitive distortions are exaggerated or irrational thoughts that form a negative lens from which we view the world. Depressed, anxious, and traumatized minds are fertile ground for warped thoughts to flourish. These thoughts feel true until you learn to recognize them as anything but. The occasional unbalanced thought is considered normal; however, when these thoughts become habitual, they can do great harm to your mood, behavior, and even your relationship with God. While the organization of cognitive distortions was born from the world of psychology, we see how learning them offers practical help in obeying Scripture's instruction to "take every thought captive" (2 Cor. 10:5) and make it obedient to Christ. Learning to recognize them is how we flip the script; it's how we align faulty thoughts from our flesh with the foundational truth of our faith.

Let's look at some of the most common cognitive distortions:

All-or-nothing thinking (black-and-white thinking)	Viewing situations in extremes, with no middle ground.	*Example:* "I lost my temper, I'm a complete failure as a mom."
Catastrophizing (Fortune telling)	Assuming the absolute worst outcome, which often results in irrational fears and anxiety.	*Example:* "My head hurts, I must have a brain tumor."
Disqualifying or discounting the positive	Ignoring, or dismissing, good things as if they don't matter, or are a fluke.	*Example:* "I got asked to lead a Bible study, but my pastor just feels sorry for me. I'm not really smart enough."
Emotional reasoning	Believing that feelings are the same as facts, and define the truth.	*Example:* "I feel unloved by God so He has probably abandoned me."
Labeling	Assigning a negative label to yourself, or others, based off of one event.	*Example:* "I didn't finish my Bible plan, I'm such a failure in life."
Magnification/ minimization	Blowing problems out of proportion, or downplaying the positive.	*Example:* "I messed up while leading worship, I'm a failure," or "I'm not that great, anyone could run the ministry."
Mental filtering	Focusing solely on the negative and disregarding the positive.	*Example:* "I disagreed with my friend over decorations, I'm a horrible ministry partner."

Mind reading	Assuming what others are thinking or feeling.	*Example:* "She didn't smile at me at church, she hates me."
Overgeneralization	Assuming one bad event means all future events will be bad, often using words like *every*, *always*, or *never*.	*Example:* "I will always feel this sad, and it will never get better."
Personalization	Taking responsibility for things that aren't your fault, or are out of your control.	*Example:* "Our event wasn't well-attended; it's totally my fault for not planning it better."
Should and must statements	Placing unrealistic expectations on ourselves or others.	*Example:* "I should always be serving other people," or "I must have perfect attendance to church."
Blaming	Accusing others of things even if they're not fully responsible.	*Example:* "My small group isn't growing because I'm not doing enough," or "God makes my life hard because I'm not perfect."

While still sitting in my closet, my time in evidence-based therapy collided with Scripture, and I recognized my scribbled thoughts to be unhealthy and not based on reality. That clarity was His light shining in my darkness, and the darkness of trauma was not overcoming it. Because I could recognize how extreme my automatic thoughts were and how they were keeping me in a negative frame of mind, I understood how, through lament, I could reframe and redirect my thoughts into prayers. Yes, I could reframe them to be more balanced, but what if I went a step further and cast those anxieties on the One who cares for me? I wasn't ignoring or pretending not to feel the despair reflected in my words, but rather than assume a fetal position in the bottom of that pit, I looked up in faith for help. Like David, whose words recorded in Psalm 18 are tied to God's rescue from his enemies, including Saul, I called to God in my distress as the ropes of death wrapped me up tight.

> The ropes of death were wrapped around me; the torrents of destruction terrified me. The ropes of Sheol entangled me; the snares of death confronted me. I called to the LORD in my distress, and I cried to my God for help. From his temple he heard my voice, and my cry to him reached his ears. (vv. 4–6)

"Now lament it," I thought again.

There was no escaping the Lord's inescapable, still, small voice. I immediately went line by line in my journal, reframing my despair into hopeful, yet still sorrowful, words of lament. Like David, I called to the Lord while in distress in my closet, and I was finally practicing this lost language of hope rather than just pondering it. Reframing, rather than repressing, became my goal, with lament being the vehicle in which I would learn to take my thoughts captive in the healthiest way possible.

Reframing, in a therapeutic sense, is the practice of looking at your circumstances from a different perspective. Oftentimes, thought patterns are based on an emotion-driven reaction to a situation. These thoughts and feelings may no longer serve you well; however, because they are deeply embedded in old patterns possibly formed from trauma, it can be hard to break them. For instance, because I feel abandoned by my dad who left me, the minute someone doesn't respond to a text, my first automatic thought is: "They are going to leave me; everyone always leaves me." This is not true;

however, in a mind that has experienced abandonment, it *feels* true. It turns my gaze from the Father and holds it captive within my current feeling, as well as my past trauma. That feeling becomes the filter from which I view the world, and sadly, all too often, the Lord. But learning to recognize these cognitive distortions is a victorious step in coping and living as the conqueror you are through Christ Jesus. Reframing is an essential step in pursuing mental health and learning that you do have more control than you may realize in what you do with the thoughts and feelings that make you feel like a hostage in your own mind and body. In that closet, I still felt a tug toward despondency, but as I reframed my words of despair into words of prayer, I experienced a renewed confidence in the Lord. Rather than peace with unbelief, I declared war. In that prayer closet, my Father trained me in lament, for simply learning about lament wasn't enough. I was beginning to see that healing would come through practicing it.

I once thought I needed to simply lament my innermost feelings, but that day I learned that it may be easier to freely express my despairing feelings in writing before I rewrite them in faith; before I strike through them. And that's essentially what I was using—strike-through. Strike-through is often used in technology and involves adding a line through certain text as an indication that it's no longer accurate or necessary. My raw journal entry seemed truthful to me as it poured onto the page; however, as I saw the distorted statements I had written, and lamented those thoughts and feelings to the Lord, my eyes of faith saw the fallacy in them. Something to ponder about strike-through is that the text isn't actually removed, but rather just crossed through. Even if emotion is a gift, overwhelming emotion may lead to unhealthy thoughts, beliefs, misunderstandings, and reactions. You can feel stuck in a loop, and feel as though you've been switched to autopilot. There are various ways out of this loop, many of which I've learned through the help of a counselor, but I also believe one way to freedom is through lament. Pausing to consider if my feelings, triggered from an emotional response to something, align with the truth of Scripture presents the option to choose faith over feelings. Because painful emotion often remains as you begin to voice hopeful trust through lament, striking through words of despair acts as a way to honor them without yielding to them. Here is an example:

Sample journal entry:

> *God has abandoned me. God makes everyone hate me. Everyone forgets me. No one cares about me, and it will never get better. I am shameful and everyone will reject me. I know the Bible says God sees my suffering, but I am invisible. I feel like trauma ruined my mind and there's no way God will heal me. God doesn't hear me. My life is hopeless. I should just die.*

Let's first pick this apart and look for cognitive distortions.

> *God has abandoned me.* (emotional reasoning)
>
> *God makes everyone hate me.* (blaming)
>
> *Everyone forgets me.* (overgeneralization)
>
> *No one cares about me* (overgeneralization), *and it will never get better* (all-or-nothing thinking).
>
> *I am shameful* (labeling) *and everyone will reject me.* (catastrophizing)
>
> *I know the Bible says God sees my suffering, but I am invisible.* (emotional reasoning)

I feel like trauma ruined my mind (emotional reasoning) *and there's no way God will heal me.* (catastrophizing)

God doesn't hear me. (emotional reasoning)

My life is hopeless. (overgeneralization)

I should just die. (should statement)

Now, let's reframe those very real and raw emotions into a prayer of lament. The goal is not to ignore painful emotions, but to recognize what their presence is indicating, and take them to the Lord in faith.

~~God has abandoned me.~~ *Lord, it feels like You have abandoned me.* ~~God makes everyone hates me.~~ *Lord, it feels like you make everyone hate me, do you?* ~~Everyone forgets me. No one cares about me, and it will never get better.~~ *It feels like everyone hates me and forgets me. Will it ever get better? Lord, help me to remember my hope and that You can do more than I ask or imagine.* ~~I am shameful and there is no way anyone could forgive me.~~ *I feel ashamed, but I know You have forgiven me. Help me to believe that. Please help others not to reject me.* ~~I know the Bible says God sees my suffering, but I am invisible.~~ *I know You are the God who sees me, but I feel invisible. Where are You? Have You forgotten me? Please show me Your love.* ~~Trauma has ruined my mind, and there's no way God will heal me.~~ *Lord, I feel like trauma has ruined my mind, but I know you are greater than trauma. Father, please heal me!* ~~God doesn't hear me.~~ *Help me feel Your nearness. Listen to me, God. Help! You are faithful, and I know I can trust You.* ~~My life is hopeless. I should just to die.~~ *I will live and sing of Your love. Thank You for giving me hope. Suicide cannot be an option; help me choose life!*

I ran to my closet ready to give up in despair, but I walked out remembering I was a daughter of the God who helps me. I was finally praying with authenticity, and I would never be the same.

By now, I hope you have a good grasp on what lament is, the various elements within a lament, and even an understanding of how to implement lament. But what I've learned over the years is that simply learning what lament is, or being told to lament, may not necessarily produce lament.

Charles Spurgeon once said, "To search out the cause of our sorrow is often the best surgery for grief. Self-ignorance is not bliss; in this case it is misery. The mist of ignorance magnifies the causes of our alarm; a clearer view will make monsters dwindle into trifles."[2] Your traumatic childhood happened, and nothing good comes from pretending it didn't. Being untethered to your story creates an incongruent conflict within because your body remembers what happened to you even if you think healing comes from pushing it away and pressing onward. In reality, healing cannot happen until we feel our pain and own our stories. *What was* is intimately connected to *what is*, and we must grieve how *what was* has affected *what is* in order to move into the hopeful territory of *what can be*.

Until you grieve your painful childhood, it's hard to thrive in adulthood. Until you grieve what your mother and father didn't give you, you cannot soar in God's freedom. The childhood wounds holding you hostage will certainly benefit from professional, trauma-informed help, but they will find their full healing in Jesus. The journey will undoubtedly include a trek through the shadowy valley of death, but remember that as you tend to your past, the Shepherd tends to you. Lament may begin in tears over wounding, but it ends in worshipful trust. And remember, we are not grieving alone when lament is our song.

As we move forward, I want you to know that as we move into discussing things such as emotional neglect and attachment trauma, complicated grief may flare up. My goal is not to cause or exasperate grief, but to show you the godly way to pray in the midst of it. If the following chapters introduce you to painful concepts you haven't considered regarding your childhood, I pray that you will seek the appropriate help from trained professionals. While I will be discussing various hindrances that could be keeping you from attaching to God emotionally, these pages are more of an introduction into what may be keeping you from intimate connection with God rather than a comprehensive guide to working through your specific trauma. So without further ado, let's investigate what may be hindering you from lamenting your pain to your Father.

Reflection Questions

1. Have you been through a trial where you were at a loss as to how God could allow such a thing?

2. If so, how did you respond?

3. What cognitive distortions do you see yourself thinking often?

Now it's your turn. Grab a journal and write your own lament. In appendix 1 you'll find words that may help you describe what you're feeling, and in appendix 2, you'll find a guide for response and prayer as you reflect on this chapter.

PART 2

Hindrances to Lament

CHAPTER 4

Emotional Neglect

*The helpless one entrusts himself to you;
you are a helper of the fatherless.*

Psalm 10:14b

Before bed, a meltdown between our three teens left us reeling, and my yelling voice joining the chaos stunned everyone. They are supposed to act like teens; I am not. In a moment of relational disaster, shame exploded in my heart. The curtain hiding my complicated childhood was pulled back without my permission, and in a matter of minutes, I recognized the voice of my own yelling dad was painfully present in mine.

Grief.

Was I trapped in an immutable destiny of being just like him? I tried to calm down, but couldn't. I had been hijacked by my inner child's invisible wounds of emotional neglect from a dad who probably didn't understand his inability to connect with me. "What happens when these immature parents lack the emotional responsiveness necessary to meet their children's emotional needs? The result is emotional neglect, a phenomenon as real as any physical deprivation."[1] It took years to recognize my upbringing as emotionally unhealthy, but the more I learned, the more I couldn't unsee it. Clarity gained meant grief experienced. I grieved what I didn't have as a child, but also that I didn't understand why I always felt so lonely inside. You see, "Children have no way of identifying a lack of emotional intimacy in their relationship with a parent. It isn't a concept they have. And it's even less likely that they can understand that their parents are emotionally immature. All they have is a gut feeling of emptiness, which is how a child experiences loneliness."[2] My gnawing loneliness was confusing, and probably offensive, to my husband whose lavish attention didn't cure it. Caught between loneliness from childhood and a loving husband in adulthood left me feeling so chaotic inside that continuing to live became a chore.

When my therapist introduced me to the idea of emotionally immature parents, I felt resistant since my parents were successful in life. Although reluctant at first, this clarity was validating regarding my past as a daughter, and empowering regarding my future as a mother. Initially calling my dad emotionally immature felt like a betrayal, and although he chose to die, I still want to be generous with my respect. There were many ways he did provide for me, and for that I am grateful. The motive behind my vulnerability is not to disrespect him or overshadow the joyful memories others may hold dear of him, but rather to shed light on how growing up in a less than nurturing home can greatly affect you, your relationships, and your ability to attach to God. My mother was wonderful; however, her fierce battle with cancer during my childhood unfortunately hindered the depth of relationship that could have been. Knowing the truth of your own story and thinking about your parents objectively is not wrong. It's incredibly brave, for "If we truly want to understand ourselves, we need to understand our history—our true history. Because the emotional residue of our past follows us."[3] Sugarcoating the truth doesn't soften the blow, but rather suffocates you as you suffer in silence.

So, what exactly are some of the characteristics of an emotionally immature parent? Their inconsistent reactions create confusion for their children. Their limited ability to emotionally connect to others stems from learning in their own childhood that certain feelings were wrong. They were either punished for their emotions, or never received guidance in how to deal with them. This solidified in their young hearts that deep emotion was dangerous. Parents who lack emotional maturity often excel in taking care of their child's physical needs; however, when it comes to matters of the heart, they seem oblivious. They withhold affection with little to no emotional availability. They may squash their child's excitement over an accomplishment by either being dismissive or simply changing the subject. A failure to encourage and validate their children is common. Rather than relating to their children with thoughtful intention, their reactive emotions create relationship strife. One of the most interesting things, when considering lament, is that those who are emotionally immature don't experience emotions that appear to contradict each other. "If people can blend contradictory emotions together, such as happiness with guilt, or anger with love, it shows that they can encompass life's emotional complexity. Experienced together, opposing feelings tame each other."[4] Lament embodies experiencing mixed emotions, as it involves both grief and hope, sorrow and joy. The act of lamenting your distress to the Lord, while holding onto hope that He is for you, not only nurtures your relationship with Him, but actively works on your behalf in developing emotional maturity.

My dad's temper in my reaction to my children displayed a blatant loss of self-control that was covered in the emotional residue from my past. We are convinced we will never be like our parents, yet like a detective finds at a crime scene, their fingerprints can be seen all over our children if we take a closer look. And we, the ones sandwiched between our parents and children, are the ones who made the transfer. If you are experiencing grief while reading this, please know that even in your sorrow, the God of hope is here inviting you to voice your pain to Him. This is where lament becomes an instrument in realigning our minds and hearts with our hopeful future as His children rather than our shadowy past as neglected children. Before we move forward, though, we must tend to the past, and it will be worth it.

While emotional immaturity in parents happens on a spectrum, the net effect really is the same. Their children feel emotionally lonely and invisible, which is as painful as being injured physically. Feeing alone can be confusing and difficult to describe, even moving some toward suicidal thoughts and behavior. Outsiders may assume the inner workings of a family are intimate and nurturing, safe and secure. But behind closed doors, children are aching for connectedness with no advocate to help them, and no one to bear witness to their pain. They feel alone without a helper.

Helpless

A child growing up in a home governed by an immature parent develops a sense of helplessness. While we know that every parent will disappoint their child at some point, children exposed to repeated emotional neglect may appear happy on the outside, but are drowning in a deep abyss of sadness, stress, depression, anxiety, grief, and isolation on the inside. "It's important to realize that childhood experiences of profound helplessness can feel traumatic, causing people to later react to adult feelings of helplessness with sensations of collapse and a feeling of 'There's nothing I can do, and no one will help me.'"[5]

This is the opposite of hope; this is despair. And while feelings of despair are reflected throughout various psalms of lament, allowing despair to have the last word isn't. In fact, as David's depression deepened, rather than turn away in his despair, he turned toward God and asked God to turn toward him. This is intimacy. David may have felt the darkness closing in, but his cry of faith was filled with hope in the God he believed would help him.

> Come quickly, LORD, and answer me,
> for my depression deepens.
> Don't turn away from me,
> or I will die. (Ps. 143:7 NLT)

In my journey of understanding my emotional neglect, I remember confessing, "I just feel helpless," during my weekly therapy session as I described how bad things seem to always happen to me. My therapist ever so gently pointed out the victim mentality visible in my words. Her diagnosis was met with offense on my part, but as I unwrapped her painful words, and saw my childhood with new eyes, I saw God's gift in her honesty. This learned helplessness is no surprise in cases of childhood emotional neglect. Through various experiences of chronic lack of control, children can adopt the belief that they are powerless to change their circumstances. This type of powerlessness naturally leads to children who either minimize their needs, repress their needs, or even passively accept situations that are unhealthy. You are free to get help, and interestingly enough, seeking help is the very way to counteract this perceived helplessness. One way to do this is through seeking help from professionals, but another avenue is through lament.

An adult groomed in childhood to believe there is no one to help them most likely won't engage in lament. In Psalm 70, an individual lament where David urgently seeks God's help and rescue from his enemies, we see a vulnerable confidence in his words that are the opposite of helplessness: "I am oppressed and needy; hurry to me, God. You are my *help* and my deliverer; LORD, do not delay" (v. 5, emphasis mine). What's more, regarding lament, is that when others see God's help in response to your hopeful, yet sorrowful, cries, they will see evidence that God keeps His promises. Your lament helps foster intimacy with God in your own life, but it also serves as a witness inviting others to see and believe in the Father who responds to His children.

Feeling helpless because no one helped you in childhood is traumatic, but even in the wake of trauma, God can be trusted, for His proven faithfulness through the generations indicates He is worthy of our trust. The English word *trust* in Hebrew, the original language of the psalms, is rich with meaning. "It expresses the feeling of safety and security that is felt when one can rely on someone or something else. It is used to show trust in God; in other people; or in things. In addition, this expression can also relate to the state of being confident, secure, without fear."[6] A child of an emotionally immature parent is not confident and does not feel safe and secure. "Without feeling safe, children cannot thrive, nor will they attach themselves to others outside the home. This leaves children isolated and in fear, which, if left untreated, can cause many mental health problems later in life."[7]

But is there another perspective of helplessness that is uniquely Christian, and filled with hope? There is, and it involves trust as seen throughout the psalms of lament. To trust God is to admit that you cannot do anything on your own; that you are absolutely helpless in your situation. To put it another way, we are choosing to lay ourselves down before the Lord in absolute dependence on Him, fully convinced that we need Him. Helplessness is at the very heart of the gospel, for while we were dead in our sin, unable to save ourselves, Jesus rescued us. We need a Savior because we are helpless to save ourselves.

One mindset of helplessness indicates trauma, the other indicates trust.

One is birthed through neglect, the other through God's proven faithfulness.

One leads to a victim mentality, the other to victorious living.

A victim is someone who has been hurt or damaged at the hands of someone else. By way of emotional neglect, you have been victimized, but *victim* is not your identity as a child of God. You are secure and you are loved; wanted and wonderfully made. So, what do we do once we recognize this learned sense of helplessness in our lives? We ask for help—over and over again if necessary. There is redemption in reclaiming the right to help that was taken from you. And we lament by bringing our urgent and desperate situations to Him no matter how uncomfortable at first, for this is how we learn to be vulnerable and intimate with our Helper. If you need help beginning, join my hopeful, yet sorrowful, cry to God, which is really a battle cry of victory:

> Hear, O LORD, when I cry with my voice!
> Have mercy also upon me, and answer me. . . .
> You have been my help;
> Do not leave me nor forsake me,
> O God of my salvation.
> When my father and my mother forsake me,
> Then the LORD will take care of me.
> (Ps. 27:7, 9b–10 NKJV)

Seen and Known

A childhood characterized by aching to be seen by an earthly father will naturally create difficulty believing the heavenly Father sees you. In Genesis, we see that Sarai could not conceive so she gave her Egyptian slave, Hagar, to her husband, Abram, as a way to build a family. Hagar conceived, strife ensued, and Hagar ran away into the wilderness. It was there in her isolation that the angel of the Lord addressed Hagar directly, and allowed her space to tell her story. He said to her, "Hagar, slave of Sarai, where have you come from and where are you going?" (Gen. 16:8). She replied that she was running away from her mistress. But then something peculiar happened. The angel of the Lord told her to return to Sarai, and submit to her. I have tried to run from my story and the aftermath of a childhood contaminated by trauma. I have had to learn to submit to my story; to face it head-on and stop running away through repressing it, dissociating from it, or dreaming of escaping it like my dad did. After an encounter with the angel of the Lord, Hagar, impressed by just how perceptive God's messenger was, says: "You are a God of seeing . . . Truly here I have seen him who looks after me" (v. 13 ESV). The least likely woman to encounter God perceived that He looked after her. If you can't imagine a dad lovingly connecting with you, noticing you, and looking after you, you may be more apt to name God the *One who ignores* rather than the *One who sees*. In the story of Hagar, you'll notice that it wasn't until Hagar was alone, desperate, abused, and helpless in the wilderness that she was able to see God's perfect attention. Maybe the wilderness was actually a gift that led to grasping what was true all along—that she was looked after by God.

Being seen is deeply connected to being known and understood. There is a detail in the story of Hagar that I don't want you to miss. When the angel of the Lord appeared to her, he said, "The LORD has *heard* your cry of affliction" (v. 11, emphasis mine). It was only after she felt *heard* that she felt *seen* by God. A child whose parent does not hear and attend to their cry will feel unseen, and will eventually stop crying. As an adult, though, we can finally use our voices. We can tell our stories to a pastor, a therapist, a mentor, a friend, a family member, but most importantly, we lament our stories to God. Trauma exposed to light loses power. Throughout the Bible, we see that God not only hears the groans of His children, but He responds to them. In Exodus, before the Israelites were delivered through the Red Sea, "The Israelites groaned because of their difficult labor, they cried out, and their cry for help because of the difficult labor ascended to God. God heard their groaning, and God remembered his covenant with Abraham, with Isaac, and with Jacob. God saw the Israelites, and God knew" (2:23b–25).

Allowing yourself to be known by God requires frightening vulnerability, especially if emotional intimacy had a negative connotation growing up, but as Curt Thompson says, "The process of being known is the vessel in which our lives are kneaded and molded, lanced and sutured, confronted and comforted, bringing God's new creation closer to its fullness in preparation for the return of the King."[8] While childhood wounds will certainly color our view of God, we must remember that our parents are not God.

> God doesn't neglect.
>
> God doesn't ignore.
>
> God doesn't forget.
>
> God isn't scared of intimacy.
>
> God isn't upset at your emotion.
>
> God is safe, attentive, responsive, and He delights in knowing those who belong to Him.
>
> But if anyone loves God, he is known by God. (1 Cor. 8:3 ESV)
>
> "I am the good shepherd. I know my own, and my own know me, just as the Father knows me, and I know the Father." (John 10:14–15a)
>
> . . . The Lord knows those who are his. (2 Tim. 2:19a)

Forgiving Your Parent

Finally seeing your upbringing accurately can initiate an onslaught of sadness, and maybe even bitterness. This is where grieving your parents' history can elicit compassion, as you may find that they themselves were not brought up in an environment that cultivated emotional intimacy. In the 1950s, at the tender age of four, my dad suddenly lost his dad in a car accident. This traumatic attachment break happened during a time when emotions were not openly discussed like they are today. I am curious how his precious four-year-old heart was nurtured as he grieved his hero. My dad went on to lose his beloved wife, my mother, to a horrific battle with cancer. Did he feel inadequate raising three kids without her? Did the cumulative loss create in him a fear of abandonment that manifested as controlling behavior regarding his children? Emotionally immature parents, at the deepest level, "act like they don't feel truly loved, making them fearful of losing status and ceasing to matter. Anxieties about abandonment and fears of being shamefully inadequate fuel their discomfort."[9] As a mother now, I can imagine the pain my sons would feel in losing their dad. As a wife, I imagine what it must have felt like to watch his spouse die a slow death. Looking at my dad's life with compassion humanized him, transforming him from a controlling dad to a broken, fearful boy in an adult exterior. A compassionate perspective taught me that grief and forgiveness can coexist, even when it involves someone whose negligence profoundly hurt you. I'm not justifying his shortcomings as a father, but I do believe my dad did the best he could with what he had.

Transformation

After our family meltdown, feeling like a failure ushered in shame, making me want to hide from everyone, including God. That's what shame does, though. "Whether it is the involution into the silence of our own minds or the literal turning away from someone with a downcast facial expression with eyes lowered, shame leads us to cloak ourselves with invisibility to prevent further intensification of the emotion."[10] Rather than turning to God, pouring out my pain, and asking for help, I turned away and focused on what happened to me in childhood. Instead of my convoluted pain twisting me toward my Father in total dependence on His grace, I felt like it violently wrapped around me and held me hostage. But just as a caterpillar (scientifically known as a larva) becomes a newly created butterfly, I was well on my way of grasping how to live as the new creation I already was through Christ, for remember that "if anyone is in Christ, he is a new creation; the old has passed away, and see, the new has come!" (2 Cor. 5:17).

The metamorphosis of a caterpillar into a butterfly may appear beautiful from the outside, but the miracle of being made new is gruesome and messy. The transformation happens at just the right time, for nothing about the process is random or rushed. In fact, there is a risk of botching the transformation if the process within the chrysalis (or cocoon for a moth) is disturbed. During the process, metamorphosis is postponed until the caterpillar has reached just the right size and appropriate stage, showing that God is never in a hurry and lovingly invested in the timing of the transformation. At just the right time, the carefully hidden-away caterpillar digests itself from the inside out, disintegrating into a soupy consistency. This seems extreme, but as the butterfly is made, and the new creation spreads its wings and takes its first flight into freedom, we see the breakdown was worth it. What's even more amazing is that butterflies and caterpillars don't just look different, they behave differently. This is what happens to us as we break down old patterns and beliefs learned in childhood. The process may be painful and leave us feeling like a soupy mess inside, but God is in control of the transformation, down to the tiniest detail. But notice, even as God is in control, just as the caterpillar has to put forth effort in the process, so we put forth effort in our journey, including asking for help from others and God. He will sustain you in your grief, strengthen you as you wait, and generously provide wisdom as you ask for it in faith. While the process may appear slow and messy, God's timing is perfect.

Breaking the Pattern

On that evening when chaos broke out between my teens, and my childhood wounds were visible for all to see, I quickly remembered that when a child acts their age, my job as the mother is to act mine. While that's easier said than done, I saw years of therapy pay off in helping me recognize that I was suddenly sixteen for a brief moment. Clarity may evoke grief, but without clarity, how do we learn to do better with our own children?

Even though grief persisted, there was victory in recognizing the problem and having the tools to emotionally regulate. But then, if I was going to parent in a way that I wasn't parented, I had to do the uncomfortable next right thing and put those learned skills of emotional maturity into practice. I could have pretended it was all fine and headed to bed, for that was my childhood experience of my dad, or I could own up to my behavior and ask for forgiveness. Asking forgiveness regarding your reaction is not saying you were wrong to be upset, it's acknowledging you could have reacted in your frustration with thought rather than without it.

With a heavy heart, I entered the hallway, only to hear sniffling from our youngest behind his closed door. He was telling his older brother how stressed out he was. It hit me like a ton of bricks that had I not heard him, I would have gone to bed and left his eight-year-old mind and heart in complete distress and, ultimately, loneliness. In that moment of hearing my son's heartbreak, God's grace empowered me to connect emotionally with him, even if I felt handicapped in doing so. What he said upon seeing me, though, has stuck with me even to this day. He admitted that he felt responsible for how I acted. What would have happened to his tender heart had he internalized his mom's lack of emotional regulation as his fault? You see, "Emotionally mature people want to be responsible for their own behavior and are willing to apologize when needed. This kind of basic respect and reciprocity mends injured trust and hurt feelings and helps maintain good relationships."[11] As I took responsibility for how I reacted, I was thankful to see how years of Bible study and therapy were collectively changing my mind and behavior. I felt grief for the little girl in me who needed what I was giving him, but that grief was tamed by joy as I experienced the miracle of God's redemption. There's always grief when you're saying no to how things were, but there's also hope for all that will be. And right there in the middle of this tension is God's invitation to pour out our hearts to Him in lament.

Reflection Questions

1. Did you experience emotional neglect as a child?

2. Have you allowed yourself to grieve unhealthy aspects of your childhood?

3. Are there any ways that your childhood has hindered your emotional intimacy with God?

Now it's your turn. Grab a journal and write your own lament. In appendix 1 you'll find words that may help you describe what you're feeling, and in appendix 2, you'll find a guide for response and prayer as you reflect on this chapter.

CHAPTER 5

Attachment

*Keep me safe, O God,
for I have come to you for refuge.*
PSALM 16:1 NLT

I nervously looked up from my coffee as my friend's compassionate smile extended the unspoken invitation to share my heart. Our time-tested friendship was tainting my ability to hide. Desperation for connection ripped the invisible duct tape off my mouth and I sheepishly admitted, "I just don't believe God loves me." The fear of being known, when you haven't felt known, is distressing. I had been tossed overboard, and the dissonance from verbalizing the very thing I worked to hide was like a weight pulling me toward the abyssal plain. God threw me a friend as a life preserver, but trauma threw me one as well. Dissociation, the well-worn way my mind had learned to cope with high levels of stress and prolonged exposure to trauma, was the life preserver I clung to rather than her words of encouragement. At the crossroads of hiding my childhood wounds and honoring them, I detached from the moment. But as I internally flailed and choked and nearly drifted under a sea of anxiety, my friend's undistracted presence and intentional eye contact grounded me, proving God's neurological design that includes our need for face-to-face communication. My childhood wounds were able to heist my hope for connection, but my friend's presence would prove vital in my eventual awakening to the comfort found within secure attachment. Insecurity silenced me from disclosing much else that evening, but hindsight illuminates that courageous confession as a baby step toward what would become a paradigm shift.

    I once described the overall anxiety, avoidance, and disconnect I felt with God by using the word *love*, when in reality, not feeling *safe* with God is a better description. Feeling *safe* and feeling *loved* are interconnected, yet the study of attachment reveals them to be conceptually distinct from one another. British psychiatrist Dr. John Bowlby originally worked with adults, but began focusing on children in the 1930s. Bowlby revolutionized the world of child psychiatry and psychology through his pioneering work that included investigating the emotional impact on a child when their bond is disrupted with their mother. His focus on understanding the lasting emotional impact of childhood separations and losses has come to be called "attachment theory." According to Bowlby, when an infant sees his mother, he will smile, vocalize sounds, and his eyes will look for her in a way that he doesn't look for others. With perceptual discrimination present, the infant recognizes his mother, tries to maintain proximity to her, and cries or attempts to follow her when she leaves the room. This is attachment behavior. "Attachment behavior has been defined as seeking and maintaining proximity to another individual,"[1] and when we seek proximity, what we're really seeking is closeness, safety, security, and protection within intimate relationships. According to Bowlby, "All forms of attachment behaviour tend to be directed towards a particular object in space, usually the special attachment-figure. In order that they be so directed it is necessary for the infant to orient towards that figure."[2] This is followed by *signaling behavior* (bringing mother to child) or *approach behavior* (bringing child to mother) in an effort to increase proximity. Like a child orients toward their parent and signals for a response, so we orient ourselves toward God and lament our pain in hopeful expectation of His response.

Attachment Behavior

Signaling behavior is seen in social signals such as an infant crying, babbling, and smiling; however, none are more compelling at bringing a mother quickly to her child than a cry of pain. When a mother hears a cry, she becomes prepared to take quick action on behalf of her child in various ways such as protecting, feeding, and comforting. Lament, by implication, is signaling behavior of the most powerful kind. Perhaps your signaling as a child fell on the deaf ears of an unresponsive parent, but your cries are always heard, and perfectly responded to, by God. Confident signaling behavior is seen in David's lament recorded in Psalm 86:

> LORD, hear my prayer;
> listen to my cries for mercy.
> I call on you in the day of my distress,
> for you will answer me. (vv. 6–7)

Not only does he cry to God (signaling), but his confidence that the Lord will answer him is surely based on the Lord's faithfulness in the past. As soon as a child becomes mobile, they typically approach and follow their mother. This behavior becomes organized on what Bowlby calls a *goal-corrected basis*, meaning that if a child realizes their mother has changed her position, they will follow her by changing direction as well. As the child matures cognitively, a child will not only approach and follow his mother, but employ every skill at his disposal to *seek* her when she is absent. Perhaps your caregiver proved unsafe to approach, and no matter how you followed or sought them out, you never found them, but that is not the case with God. In God's wisdom and careful sanctification of His children, He may feel distant at times, but He never forsakes. Jeremiah 29:13 says: "Then you will seek Me, inquire for, *and* require Me [as a vital necessity] and find Me when you search for Me with all your heart" (AMPC). Just as a parent is a vital necessity to a child, God is a vital necessity to us, who will be found when we seek Him. And one of the most honest and healthy ways we can seek Him, and find Him, is by lamenting through the dimmed lens of depression we struggle to see and feel Him through.

Attachment Trauma

Bowlby's pioneering work in attachment theory suggests that we are biologically designed to create and maintain attachments with other people. In an ideal world, a child grows up in a family that cultivates a culture of protection, connection, responsiveness, play, and consistency. Ideally, a child's signaling behavior will elicit a response from their parent, solidifying in their growing understanding of the world that they are safe and cared for. But what happens when a child's pursuit of proximity repeatedly proves unfruitful? While emotionally immature parents, as discussed in the previous chapter, can evoke a host of difficulty within their child, one of the most profound wounds they can inflict, even if unintentional, is attachment trauma. When a caregiver lacks emotional maturity, they tend to parent from a place of their own trauma, whether it be early abuse, their own attachment wounds as children, or even simply the natural loss of a secure attachment that wasn't processed in a healthy way. Trauma is the result of an experience in which you had little control over what happened, and felt a profound sense of helplessness. A child who experiences a break in secure attachment feels utterly disconnected from everything and everyone, including God.

As a parent themselves, trauma controls and preoccupies them and, in turn, traumatizes you by their lack of healthy response to your needs. The blueprint laid by our earliest bonds have a tremendous impact on our entire life, our relationships, and as I am suggesting in this chapter, our ability to flourish in an intimate, securely attached relationship with God. And isn't that what our entire faith is based on? While understanding this may induce grief, gaining clarity regarding the lingering effect our early attachments have on our current relationships becomes a conduit of change. Knowledge offers opportunity for growth, but with that comes grief. The journey of turning from childhood wounds in hope begins with a turning toward them in sorrow, considering how your childhood has birthed ongoing insecurity with others.

As we dive into the various styles of attachment, we must look at what attachment isn't. Your attachment style isn't a personality type or a product of being an optimist or a pessimist. It also doesn't reflect a life of ease or ongoing perfection. Attachment is about feeling safe, taken care of, and having the support of someone on your side. On the surface, attachment may be misunderstood as simply bonding, but they aren't quite the same. Attachment and bonding both describe the feelings between and baby and parent, but attachment is about building a relationship over time that produces a child who feels safe, secure, loved, and ready to venture out into the world. Bonding, on the other hand, is all about the parent. It refers to the surge of love and tenderness that is felt by the parent. Yes, if a parent fails to bond with their child, the child will be less likely to attach to their parent, but bonding and attachment focus on different perspectives of the early parent-infant relationship. "Attachment theory describes essentially how the child builds up a relationship with its primary caregiver and bonding theory describes the feelings, thoughts, and behaviors of the parent towards the baby."[3]

Even if you never quite felt bonded with your parents during your childhood, and you were insecurely attached as well, God is perfectly bonded with His children, which lays the groundwork for our secure attachment to Him. Because our relational history helps, or hinders, us in grasping our relationship with God, He graciously offers practical examples in Scripture that invite us to better understand His attentive care. For example, the Lord says, "Can a woman forget her nursing child, or lack compassion for the child of her womb? Even if these forget, yet I will not forget you" (Isa. 49:15). Here, "The most vivid and poignant image of God's commitment to his people is expressed in a rhetorical question involving mothers and children. A mother should always love and cherish her child; normally it is unthinkable that she would forsake her. Yet sad cases do occur of neglected and abandoned children, which are all the more shocking because of their unnaturalness. But even if some mothers behave in this way, God never will. The love of the Lord exceeds even the most tender of earthly loves (cf. Ps. 27:10)."[4] A bonded parent is a mindful parent, and there is no one more mindful of you than the One who created you. In learning to trust God as an emotionally safe attachment figure, we must remember who He is. He is bonded with you and, even in all His greatness, His mindfulness is astonishing, for "When I look at your heavens, the work of your fingers, the moon and the stars, which you have set in place, what is man that you are mindful of him, and the son of man that you care for him?" (Ps. 8:3–4 ESV).

If you've noticed an anxious or avoidant bent in your behavior with others, I'm guessing it's there with God too. This is why it's important to bring these patterns out of the darkness, where diseased perceptions of God infect our lives, and into the light, where healing begins. You can't change what happened to you, but the patterns from your past that continue to show up in the present can change. Not only does the world of psychology attest to this, but as a child of God, you are filled with the resurrection power of Christ that can accomplish what others deem impossible. As we dive further into the world of attachment, I pray that you will practice compassion with yourself. Your insecure attachment style was developed through attachment adaptation. A baby is born needing parents in order to survive, but when parents display limitations, that same baby must adapt for their own survival, even shutting off their need for connection. This speaks to the remarkable way children will adapt to whatever situation they are born into. If this is your story, I believe your adaptation deserves recognition, for it shows that you don't give up easily. It doesn't negate the need for secure attachment you were born with, but it does highlight your resilience. The fact that you even needed to be resilient in the first place most likely washes you in grief waiting to be lamented to your loving Father. You may loathe the insecure attachment style you feel locked into, but no attachment style is immutable. There is hope.

Secure Attachment

Although Dr. Bowlby receives most of the credit for developing attachment theory, his student and eventual colleague, Mary Ainsworth, built upon his theory through her famous "Strange Situation" experiment. During this experiment, an infant was separated from their parent or caregiver for a brief amount of time, and then closely observed as they were reunited. How the infant acted upon reunification spoke to their internal understanding of intimate relationships, and led to the children being categorized into attachment styles. Her work made a lasting impression on psychology, and the attachment styles she developed, including the ideal secure attachment, are still used today. Adult attachment expert Diane Poole Heller, PhD, explains in her book, *The Power of Attachment*: "Although secure attachment can sound out of reach or like a fantasy goal for many of us, it's how we are fundamentally designed to operate. No matter how unattainable it seems, secure attachment is always there, just waiting to be uncovered, recalled, practiced, and expressed."[5] And that one evening with my friend, when I doubted God's love, I was uncovering and practicing the secure attachment I would eventually learn to embody. It was uncomfortable, but as a plant reaches for the light, growing up from its buried existence in the dark, my yearning for connection reached for my friend, which would prove the rehearsal for my eventual orientation toward God. I may still lean toward insecurity with others; however, over time, I continue to see that practice makes progress. Once you begin to experience secure attachment with others, you will see that, when stressed, you don't have to automatically follow the insecurely attached feelings, thoughts, and tendencies that have been your automatic response for years. "Your nervous system doesn't get stressed out about being close to people, which frees you from needing to defend against unwanted anxiety triggered by closeness and intimacy."[6]

You see, your nervous system is the way God designed messages to travel from your brain to all the other parts of your body, alerting your body how to behave. Think of it as your body's command center. These messages are an automatic response that tell your body to do all kinds of things including sleep and breathe. It also regulates things like thoughts, feelings, learning, aging, and sweating in the midst of a stressful situation. Your nervous system's response to a reminder of past trauma is not sinful, but rather how God designed your body to work and respond automatically. For example, if your mother caused attachment trauma in your life, then an older woman at church initiating a friendship with you may trigger you, sending you into a trauma response such as fight, flight, or freeze. This is an example of how attachment trauma may be felt physically.

Learning to recognize when your nervous system has become dysregulated means there is hope for employing coping skills, which I have learned through spending time in therapy. You can love Jesus, read the Bible, pray, serve, live in community, and yet because of past trauma, still experience your nervous system becoming dysregulated in a moment of being reminded of what has happened to you. Lament is the way to voice that frustration to God in hope that even if your body continues to cause sorrow on earth, you can trust and rely on Him as your safe haven. Lament acknowledges the grief trauma has caused on your body, yet looks forward in expectation to the day in God's presence that you will no longer be bound by a body that frustrates you.

Secure Attachment to Others

Secure attachment is the goal. Those who are secure have a greater capacity to think and process whatever comes their way. While secure attachment sounds like a dream, we mustn't romanticize it, as no one is immune to difficult relationships or feeling insecure with others. Secure people, though, will bounce back quicker and even learn from whatever wasn't ideal. Unlike emotionally immature people, those who are securely attached can communicate their wants, needs, emotions, hopes, and dreams. When there is a problem, they have the mental fortitude to focus on the problem rather than attacking those who are involved in it. They are invested in repairing relational ruptures and tend to be flexible, good with boundaries, supportive, and nourishing to others. They embrace the benefits of close relationships such as feeling safe, protected, satisfied, and secure, yet don't fear being alone.

Secure Attachment to God

A securely attached child will not only feel safe and supported, but they will cultivate connections with their caregivers. This connection enables them to express their emotions, as well as return to their parent as a home base when they need comfort and protection. A child of God, who understands His character, will enjoy safety in their relationship with Him, for "the Lord is faithful, and he will strengthen you and protect you from the evil one" (2 Thess. 3:3 NIV). They will easily find refuge in the Lord and will feel comfortable lamenting to God. The beauty of an adult who loves and reverently fears the Lord is that not only will they be secure, but their children are more likely to follow suit. This is seen in Proverbs 14:26 NLT: "Those who fear the LORD are secure; he will be a refuge for their children."

If we look for it, secure attachment can be seen in Scripture, with psalms of lament being one of the easiest places to look for it. These laments were gifted to us by a God who invites us to voice the sorrow we carry. The following psalm offers us a template and vocabulary to adopt as our very own cry of hopeful sorrow.

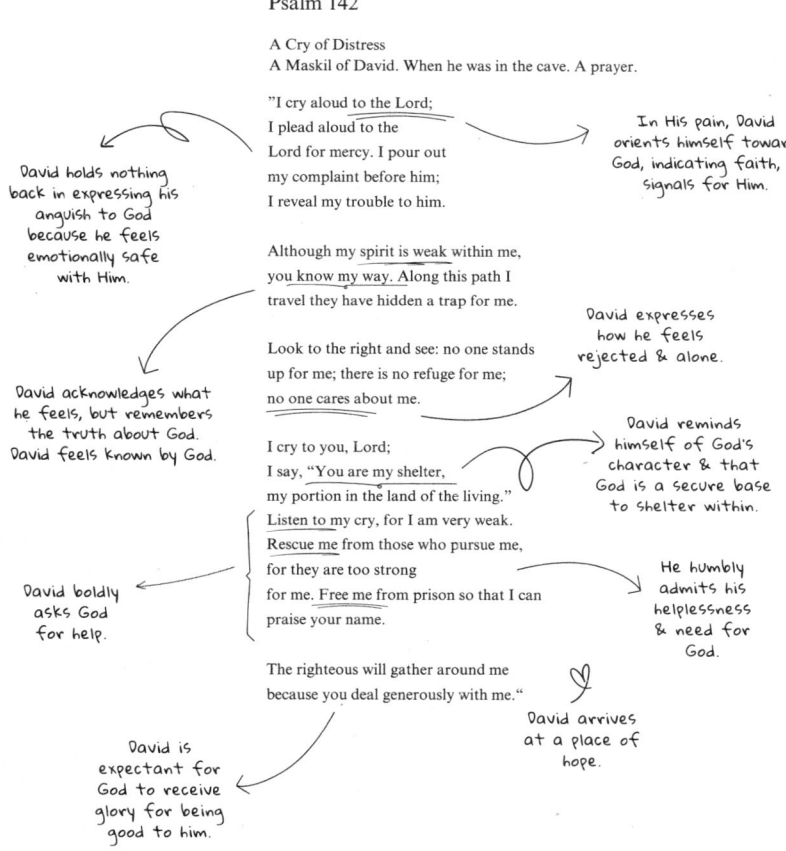

Anxious Attachment to Others

Anxious attachment, also referred to as preoccupied attachment, anxious-preoccupied attachment, or anxious-ambivalent attachment, looks like fearing abandonment or rejection. Children with an anxious attachment have caregivers who are unable to read their child, often because they struggle to see past their own anxiety. A child in this type of situation finds it hard to predict their parent's behavior when it comes to their availability and responsiveness. An anxious attachment often leaves a child wanting intimacy with their caregiver, even going to them for comfort, yet as the parent attempts to comfort them, they may prove inconsolable and afraid to leave their parent. People with an anxious attachment may also feel jealous, suffer from low self-esteem, have a hard time setting boundaries, experience high sensitivity to criticism, desire constant reassurance of love, struggle with codependency, and worry about losing their loved ones.

Anxious Attachment to God

Someone who displays an anxious attachment to God may feel unworthy of His love. Their self-esteem may be so low that it's hard to grasp their identity in Christ. They may desire intimacy with God, yet also fear being abandoned or rejected by Him. Due to high sensitivity to criticism, they may worry about losing their salvation and experience stress at the thought of being convicted by the Holy Spirit. Because those with an anxious attachment will filter Scripture through this attachment pattern, they may sense God to be unreliable like their parents were. If you believe God is unreliable, lamenting your pain and trusting Him to come to your aid most likely wouldn't even cross your mind. Psalms of lament may be difficult to utilize as a prayer guide if anxiety dominates your thoughts and feelings regarding relationships.

If anxiety characterizes your attachment to God, consider lamenting in this way:

> *O Lord, I want to trust You, but I can't. Why do You feel so distant and unavailable sometimes? Why didn't You give me someone when I was a child who helped me feel safe? Scripture tells me that Your name is a strong tower that the righteous can run to for safety (Prov. 18:10); help me believe and practice this. I*

trust You, for You are steadfast in love and full of mercy.

Avoidant Attachment to Others

Avoidant attachment style, also referred to as *dismissive attachment* or *anxious-avoidant attachment*, may look like avoiding intimacy within relationships and having a hard time trusting others. It's possible for children with an avoidant attachment style to have parents who love them and do their best to provide for their needs, yet remain emotionally unavailable for them. Despite a parent's concern for the child's welfare, their unresponsiveness, or outright rejection of a child's emotional state, communicates that feelings don't matter. A child who adapts by detaching from emotion will then avoid intimacy with others. Someone who is avoidant may struggle with commitment, feel threatened when others attempt to become intimate, have difficulty expressing needs, suppress their emotions, and have a strong sense of independence.

Avoidant Attachment to God

Someone who displays an avoidant attachment to God may struggle trusting and being intimate with Him. They may feel threatened when Scripture speaks of God's love, and struggle to commit to Him. Psalms of lament may be difficult to resonate with if sharing their innermost thoughts and feelings with others is uncomfortable. They may even be so detached from their emotions, that knowing how to verbalize what they feel could seem out of reach. Another aspect of lament that may be hindered is boldly asking God for help, or even understanding the concept of being dependent on God.

If avoidance characterizes your attachment to God, consider lamenting in this way:

> *God, it feels like You provide for my physical needs, but that my heart is all alone in this world. Why? Why do You feel so aloof to what is happening and like You don't care? I hate that my dad was distant and seemed to avoid emotional closeness with me. Help me to trust You and stop avoiding You. Help me to hunger for Your Word, for I know it is how the Spirit transforms me and renews my mind. I love You and am choosing to trust that You are the God Who Sees Me (Gen. 16:13).*

Disorganized Attachment to Others

Disorganized attachment style, also referred to as *fearful-avoidant attachment,* is the most extreme of the attachment styles, and looks like displaying confusing or contradictory behaviors. A child who has developed disorganized attachment to their parents will both love and fear them, because they have failed to provide a safe and secure base for them to return to. This chaotic understanding of their caregiver leaves the child fearing rejection and abandonment. Someone with disorganized attachment may also have trouble regulating their own emotions, difficulty being vulnerable with others, feel unlovable or unworthy of love, and desire emotional closeness while pushing others away.

Disorganized Attachment to God

Someone with disorganized attachment to God may seek intimacy with Him, but then also try to run from Him. They may find it hard to believe Scripture that speaks of God's love or describes Him as a refuge and strong tower, and live in fear that He will reject them. Lamenting their pain may prove difficult if vulnerability with others is challenging. Utilizing the language found in the psalms of lament would be uncomfortable due to a chaotic experience with others and lack of understanding of relational safety. They may desire emotional closeness with God, but feel compelled to push Him away. Their inconsistent caregivers may influence them to believe God changes, although Malachi 3:6a ESV says, "For I the LORD do not change."

If disorganization and confusion characterizes your attachment to God, consider lamenting in this way:

> *Lord, one minute I feel You close, but then it's like You go away. Where are You? Did I do something wrong? Help me, Lord. I want to believe You won't reject me. I feel chaotic inside. Help me to trust You, and others, with my heart. Help me not to fear losing You. James 1:17 tells me that You are the Father of lights who does not change like shifting shadows. I am choosing to trust You in my darkness. It feels like it will never get better, but hope in Christ means it will. Thank You for being the light that will never be overcome.*

If this chapter has been an eye-opening introduction into how your childhood has shaped your attachment to God, it is normal for intense emotion to surface, or even to experience numbness from the trauma of it all. But maybe this isn't new information, and rather just a reminder of the grief that you carry. In either case, we must remember God is the God of reversals and there is no pain of childhood that cannot find comfort in Him. Even though we may be adults housing hurting, lonely, and even abandoned children within us, the truth is that we are loved, held, and protected by God. When parents fail to protect, God fiercely does. When parents fail to notice, God has His loving eye on you.

Lamenting Attachment Trauma

Perfection is not a prerequisite for fostering secure attachment in your child, as no parent is perfect, but parents do bear a weighty calling in creating the worldview from which their child will first relate to God. Throughout Scripture, we see Jesus explain the Kingdom through ordinary examples such as bread, fire, sheep, and soil, and through familial roles such as describing God as a father to His born-again children. God said, "And I will be a Father to you, and you will be sons and daughters to me" (2 Cor. 6:18); however, this beautiful benefit of salvation can be a hard pill to swallow when you have grown up in a difficult relationship with one or more of your parents. The Father searching and knowing you (Ps. 139:1) feels uncomfortable. Believing God will never leave nor forsake you (Heb. 13:5) feels unfathomable. While understandable, what if rather than projecting our parents' shortcomings onto God, we could see Him for who He really is? He will never neglect, abuse, or abandon. He will never die or be aloof to whatever ails you.

Without facing our childhood wounds, though, we continue to allow our personal experience to contaminate our communion with the Lord. Praying as a way to foster a secure attachment may prove difficult if you are carrying around unprocessed trauma that has altered how you experience the world. The engrained anxious, avoidant, or disorganized attachment styles you operate from may mean you relate to Him in an anxious, avoidant, or disorganized way. In an attempt to be intimate with God, you may pour your heart out to Him, but did you know that the one who believes God will hear and respond to their prayers will have a vastly different experience than the one who cries out to God with the underlying belief that He is unavailable?

Considerable research has investigated how religion affects mental health, but one such study "adds to the literature in this area by addressing two main questions: (1) Is the frequency of prayer associated with symptoms of anxiety-related disorders among US adults? (2) Is this association conditional on the nature of individuals' attachment to God?"[7] While the study proved consistent with previous studies in showing that there doesn't seem to be a noteworthy association between psychiatric symptoms and the frequency of prayer, they did find "consistent interactions between the frequency of prayer and secure attachment to God, such that persons who pray often to a God who is perceived as a secure attachment figure derive clear mental health benefits, while those who pray to a God who is perceived as distant or unresponsive experience elevated levels of anxiety related symptoms."[8] Their scientific study also explains the association between praying to God, who is perceived to be a secure attachment figure, and experiencing security in the midst of distress. But here was the interesting part of their study when considering lament, which is a turning toward God and pouring out your pain to a responsive Father: "Persons who pray in an attempt to forge a relationship with a divine other, but who believe that their prayers are unmet, and that God is distant and unresponsive, are likely to feel a deep sense of estrangement from God's love."[9] Distant and unresponsive. Does that resonate? Science validates what Scripture reveals to be true: our belief matters. You can try to forge a relationship with God through lament, but if you perceive God as anything other than a safe haven, exposing your intimate emotions to Him could be distressing.

One of the primary characteristics of attachment involves whether or not someone sees their attachment figure as a place of security from which they venture out and explore the world, yet return to as a haven of safety when they need support, protection, and comfort in the midst of distress. Perhaps attachment theory calls this idea of a caregiver being a secure base in the world a *safe haven*, but the idea is clearly seen in psalms of lament through David's repeated description of God as his refuge. When pursued by enemies, he sought refuge in God. And while these psalms may have a wide variety of circumstances surrounding them, the idea of God as a place of safety to hide within is applicable to us in our unique circumstances as well.

> Lord my God, I seek refuge in you;
> save me from all my pursuers and rescue me.
> (Ps. 7:1)

> Lord, I seek refuge in you;
> let me never be disgraced. (Ps. 31:1a)

> Look to the right and see:
>   there is none who takes notice of me;
> no refuge remains to me;
>   no one cares for my soul.

> I cry to you, O Lord;
>   I say, "You are my refuge,
>   my portion in the land of the living."
> (Ps. 142:4–5 ESV)

The lack of safety and support you perceived from your caregiver falsely informed you that God is unsafe and unsupportive. Of course the Holy Spirit doesn't need modern psychology to transform minds, but God does use means such as medication, exercise, nutritious food, or supplements to improve our quality of life. While brilliant minds in the field of psychology may be credited for attachment discoveries, let's not lose sight of God being the creator of attachment (Gen. 2:18). Within the creation narrative, the need for connection with others is explicitly stated, but even before God created human connection, the triune God existed and operated in perfect connection. And from that perfect relationship flows all other connection—with others, but most importantly, with God. The story of Scripture happens within relationship—some healthy, and some not so much—and when studied, really can shift relational patterns so that we can walk in the light, rather than remain locked in the dark dungeon of childhood. God created marriage, friendship, and family to be experienced with others, but God also created various ways we relate to Him. In Him, orphans find a father, widows find a provider, the scared find a safe haven, and the abandoned find a companion. If we can understand why we are inclined to view God as distant, abusive, or neglectful (the opposite of Scripture's revelation), then we can begin to securely attach to Him. Uncovering the past certainly involves grief over what happened to you, but lament is the practical way to practice secure attachment to Him. It may feel uncomfortable at first, but as past wounds are processed and the Spirit renews your mind through Scripture, new pathways in your brain will form and intimacy with God will be possible.

There Is Hope for Healing

While you may be experiencing grief as we are diving deep into your childhood and making devastating discoveries regarding how trauma, neglect, or abuse has affected every relationship in your life, there is hope because of something called neuroplasticity. God's miraculous design includes brains that possess the ability to change. Neuroplasticity, in simple terms, is the brain's ability to adapt, reorganize, and even grow neural pathways due to experience. Today's understanding of this is exciting because while in the past people believed that at a certain age the brain was fixed, we now know that the brain never stops changing in response to learning. "Keep in mind that neuroplasticity is part of the design of our nervous system. So while it's true that far too many of us were raised by parents who carried old wounds of their own childhood and the suffering of their ancestors—wounds that never quite healed and caused our parents (and theirs) to struggle their entire lives—it's also true that our attachment adaptations are not written in stone."[10] Even if you feel the weight of your place within a legacy of trauma, your innate neuroplasticity is a gift from God, and when coupled with the transforming Word of God and nurturing relationships with safe loved ones, there is no limit to the mental and relational health you can grow into.

Curt Thompson, MD, touches on how attachment patterns can change in his book, *Anatomy of the Soul*: "Through a process called earned secure attachment, people can develop the sense of well-being and confidence that results from healthy attachment . . . It won't happen, though, simply because they take in new factual information or have strong willpower. This transformation requires either a significant encounter with an outside relationship or a profound change in circumstances."[11] God used my friend mentioned in the beginning of this chapter profoundly in my journey of transformation. Of course, I have had to learn facts about attachment and put forth effort to pursue mental health, but it was her consistent presence and loving acceptance that whet my appetite for secure attachment with others, and more importantly, with my Father. It didn't stop with her, though. One by one, God brought others into my life who would willingly initiate nurturing friendships with me. My initial reaction was always one of distress, even with a smile on my face. Anxiety assumed they would see the real me and leave, and avoidance sought to protect me from eventual abandonment.

But the longer I sat in the discomfort, trusting the healing power found within relationships that both science and Scripture attest to, the more secure I became. These friends, along with my loving husband, and even my consistent therapist, generated contingency with me.

In the context of attachment, "Contingency refers to a relational experience in which you feel understood by another person. You have a felt sense that this person is attuned to you, that they resonate with who you are. You feel they 'get' you. You *get gotten* and *feel felt*, so to speak."[12] This deep sense of connection is only possible because they made a point to get what was going on with me. Because of this, I learned to feel safe and relaxed. The loneliness I felt in childhood was seemingly undone one stich at a time with the seam ripper of nurturing love. This sense of contingency meant I finally felt that I had people to depend on and seek support from when I needed it. Not only is this evidence of secure attachment, but a sense of contingency with them rewrote my childhood blueprint and I no longer felt hindered in seeking support from God through lament. Experiencing people on my side helped me to confidently believe "If God is for us, who is against us?" (Rom. 8:31). As a daughter who finally saw God as a secure attachment figure, I began lamenting. "I called to the Lord in distress; the Lord answered me and put me in a spacious place. The Lord is for me; I will not be afraid" (Ps. 118:5–6a).

The implications of attachment theory are profound when looking at what may be hindering your ability to attach to God in a secure way. Recovery from attachment trauma always begins with pain, but so does lament. Allow yourself to grieve what you weren't given as a child, but remember that lament is not just sorrowful, it's also hopeful. It's the cry of faith to a loving Father who safely holds your pain in the palm of His hands, where He holds you too.

Reflection Questions

1. What are your thoughts on attachment theory?

2. Which attachment style do you feel fits you best?

3. Have you ever considered how your attachment style with others may be affecting your attachment to God?

Lamenting can be uncomfortable when attachment trauma is present. Here is an example from my own prayer life as someone who knows relational hurt, but who hopes in God:

> *Lord, why do You feel so far away? I want to trust You, but I worry that You will let me down. I'm so scared that if I tell You how I really feel, You will leave me. Why is this my story? Why do others grow up feeling safe, seen, and known, but I didn't? Don't You love me? Please help me to settle into You as my safe haven. My heart hurts, but my hope is in You. You have never let me down and are forever faithful. "Why are you cast down, O my soul, and why are you in turmoil within me? Hope in God; for I shall again praise him, my salvation and my God" (Ps. 42:11 ESV). In Christ's name, amen.*

Now it's your turn. Grab a journal and write your own lament. In appendix 1 you'll find words that may help you describe what you're feeling, and in appendix 2, you'll find a guide for response and prayer as you reflect on this chapter.

CHAPTER 6

Fear of Abandonment

Lord, do not abandon me;
my God, do not be far from me.

Psalm 38:21

"If you get a job, you're no longer my daughter." This was the jarring response I received from my dad upon sharing my plans. Surely my dad's reasoning was rational in his mind; however, he failed to convey it within the confines of unconditional love. In that moment, my fluid understanding regarding faithful love was congealed, calibrating my life with a covenant of works rather than grace. His steadfastness hinged on my behavior; it was contingent on whether or not my actions met his expectations. I didn't speak back for fear of losing what stability my dad did offer. I don't share this out of spite, but rather in the spirit of uncovering what may be hindering you from turning securely to the God who said, "I will never [under any circumstances] desert you [nor give you up nor leave you without support, nor will I in any degree leave you helpless], nor will I forsake *or* let you down *or* relax My hold on you [assuredly not]!" (Heb. 13:5 amp).

As my behavior challenged my dad's sense of control, threatening abandonment brought me back in line. To abandon means "to withdraw protection, support, or help from,"[1] and because fear is a powerful weapon, threatening to withdraw forever, which abandonment implies, is effective. The tongue, after all, is a powerful whip. "It is a restless evil, full of deadly poison" (James 3:8b), and threatening abandonment poisons the security of its recipient. "When the threat of abandonment is real, the body releases certain neurotransmitters and hormones, such as cortisol and adrenaline. In addition to this, with a lack of connection, the hormone oxytocin a feel good bonding chemical is depleted. This brain chemical reaction causes the victim to feel terrible. She will do anything to bring back the good feelings."[2] And the way I brought back the good feelings was to submit and try to secure my place as his daughter.

My obedience wasn't out of reverence, but rather from a fear of punishment. "There is no fear in love; instead, perfect love drives out all fear, because fear involves punishment. So the one who fears is not complete in love" (1 John 4:18). John expected his readers to know that someday they would stand before God and give account of themselves. Resting in the love of God provides confidence for that day. At first glance, 1 John 4:18 seemingly says that love and fear cannot coexist; however, a right understanding of fear in this context removes confusion. Here, "John is affirming that love casts out fear of rejection or condemnation in judgement. We cannot know that someone completely loves us while also fearing that he will reject us. When we fear that another will reject us, we fear that his love is not complete."[3]

John goes on to say that "We love because he first loved us" (v. 19). John explicitly states where love begins, and it begins with God. Is it any different with parents and children? A child who feels seen, heard, and cared for will translate that as being loved. These moments are like building blocks stacked on top of each other, increasing the child's capacity for love. "The attentive, loving behaviors grow the neural networks that allow us to feel love, and then act in loving ways toward others. If you are loved, you learn to love."[4]

To understand the gospel is to recognize the lies believed by those whose parents' negligent words brainwashed them to believe God doesn't love them and will leave them. God doesn't love you because of your behavior, or because you have something to offer Him, for God has no needs. God also doesn't love you because you first loved Him, and He even loves you even when you don't love Him. An emotionally immature parent who punishes you by inflicting emotional pain not only preaches the opposite of God's love, but shares manipulative characteristics of the Enemy. Not only do we love God because He first loved us, but loving our neighbors and enemies alike is a direct reflection of our being loved by God. Being emotionally neglected as a child does not excuse your obligation to love your neighbor as yourself. However, a negative childhood certainly creates friction when grasping just how loved you are by God, whom your ability to love flows from.

The word translated as "love" in 1 John 4:19 is the word *agape*, a sacrificial love that continues regardless of the circumstance. Agape is an expression of selflessness that desires the highest good for its recipient and transcends mere feeling through an emphasis on commitment and benevolence. This "Love of benevolence is not based on the loveliness of the object of the love, but rather your good will—benevolence—your good will toward the person or the thing that you are loving. Your aim in that kind of love is to do good, to bring about something beautiful, not respond to beauty."[5] Parents who only respond to you lovingly when your behavior displays beauty are not a complete picture of the benevolent, steadfast love of God. A. W. Tozer once said, "Fear is the painful emotion that arises at the thought that we may be harmed or made to suffer. This fear persists while we are subject to the will of someone who does not desire our well-being. The moment we come under the protection of one of good will, fear is cast out."[6] David's lament in Psalm 57, based on how Saul treated him, models for us seeking protection from God, whose goodwill He clung to when others expressed ill will toward him.

> Be gracious to me, God, be gracious to me,
> for I take refuge in you.
> I will seek refuge in the shadow of your wings
> until danger passes.
> I call to God Most High,
> to God who fulfills his purpose for me.
> He reaches down from heaven and saves me,
> challenging the one who tramples me.
> (Ps. 57:1–3a)

Nothing can separate you from the love of God, not even the powers of hell (Rom. 8:38–39). It's amazing how much power parents have over their child's perception of the permanence of God's love, though. My dad's behavior toward me was a weapon of unrighteousness (Rom. 6:13) used by the Enemy to shape how I related to a father—to *the* Father. It can still be hard to lament to God while having no experiential knowledge of confiding in a dad. Still bound by my fallen body and mind on earth, I grieve my bent toward fear, and therefore, I lament:

> *O Lord, why didn't You give me a dad who delighted in me? I feel unworthy of love. I'm tired of being scared You will leave me like he did. How long will I feel this way? Free me from fear, and guard my heart and mind with Your peace. I trust You, for You are faithful. I know You can use my pain for Your glory.*

In *The Soul of Shame*, Curt Thompson MD, says, "Humans tend to experience no greater distress than when in relationships of intentional, unqualified abandonment—abandoned physically and left out of the mind of the other."[7] The threat of abandonment proves distressing as well. Perhaps there are various theories as to what causes the fear of abandonment; however, "Generally, psychologists attribute fear of abandonment to experiences, beliefs, and concepts we internalize as children. A child who is denied basic, necessary comforts such as physical affection, emotional connection, and safety learns not to trust the permanence of these in adulthood."[8]

It may seem obvious that emotional neglect, abuse, or divorce may promote a fear of abandonment within a child; however, I believe it noteworthy that the natural death of a parent can create the same end: a child who fears being left. My mom's delight in motherhood wasn't enough to escape disease. Cancer confiscated her life—and my primary secure attachment along with it. Why would God take her, and leave me with a dad who threatened to take himself from me? Rather than lamenting my confusion to Him, I stuffed those heavy emotions deep down. Repressed emotions reverberated through my heart and mind, spilling over into my behavior. Hypervigilant and alone, rather than tell God about it, I pretended it wasn't so. Instead of walking by faith, I focused on what I saw: A submissive daughter is a cherished daughter. A perfect daughter is a precious daughter. A controllable daughter is a wanted daughter.

It's easy to stay angry at your parents, but lamenting anger is an avenue to forgiveness and, ultimately, compassion. Uncovering the *why* of my dad's behavior has helped me see him through the eyes of Christ, because God loves my dad too. It doesn't excuse his behavior, but it helps me see that his threats were never about me in the first place. My dad's loss of his dad in a car accident surely destroyed the idyllic notion that parents don't leave. I wonder if his threats to leave me were from the four-year-old within him whose painful loss hijacked his adult rationality when triggered. In his case, the child left behind by his dad's accidental death grew up and left behind his children by purposeful death. I don't know the emotional climate of each generation before me in my family tree, but I can look at the way my dad handled emotions, conflict, and relationships, and speculate. Speaking of trees, imagine how the multitude of roots, from various trees in a forest, eventually twist around one another underground like a twisty tie used to close up a loaf of bread. Similarly, the emotional and behavioral patterns of our ancestors get twisted up with us, influencing our emotional and behavioral patterns. What I'm describing is known as *multigenerational transmission*.

The multigenerational transmission process, developed by psychiatrist Murray Bowen, suggests that "Families pass on behaviors, emotions, and relationship patterns from generation to generation. These inherited traits can influence how we view relationships, manage stress, and approach life's challenges. Many find themselves replicating family behaviors without fully understanding why, and this concept helps explain why patterns repeat."[9] Regarding God, if your ancestors did not manage stress in a godly way, why would you be inclined to? If your parents ignored grief, or numbed it, through unhealthy coping mechanisms, lamenting to God as the way you grieve wouldn't be your first instinct. Breaking family patterns must begin with recognizing and understanding them. This is the goal of my book and, hopefully, through an introduction to what may be keeping you from connecting to God, you will then know how to turn to Him, as well as trauma-informed, trained professionals, for help. As a mom, I have struggled admitting I need help for fear of disappointing my children. But the most loving thing you can do for your children, and even your future grandchildren and great-grandchildren, is to fight for mental and relational health. Even the smallest step of differentiation between you and your parents can have lasting changes for generations to come. How we experienced our parents is likely to be repeated in how our children experience us. It's all connected like a chain. But God breaks chains and leads prisoners out with singing (Ps. 68:6 NIV).

Through the resurrection of Christ, powerful patterns of generational sin are broken, and believers are empowered to live in a way that conforms with the character of God, including being the one to change the trajectory of a family. Peter said:

> So prepare your minds for action and exercise self-control. Put all your hope in the gracious salvation that will come to you when Jesus Christ is revealed to the world. So you must live as God's obedient children. Don't slip back into your old ways of living to satisfy your own desires. You didn't know any better then. But now you must be holy in everything you do, just as God who chose you is holy. For the Scriptures say, "You must be holy because I am holy."
>
> And remember that the heavenly Father to whom you pray has no favorites. He will judge or reward you according to what you do. So you must live in reverent fear of him during your time here as "temporary residents." For you know that God paid a ransom to save you from the empty life you inherited from your ancestors. (1 Pet. 1:13–18a NLT)

Your mind won't be ready for action when it's ignoring unprocessed trauma and stuck in fight-or-flight. In an attempt to find freedom from behavior engraved in you by your parents, appeal to the Father, lament, and as His child, ask Him for help. "Although it may seem odd for Peter to speak of living in 'fear' of one's 'Father,' he does not mean by this to be afraid or live in doubt or anxiety about one's relationship with God. The emphasis is on reverence, awe, and an ever-present sense of utter dependency on the Lord's power and mercy. Thus to 'fear' God means to be conscious of his all-pervasive presence and our absolute, moment-by-moment dependence on him for light and life."[10] Engaging in lament is an expression of your dependence on God. Maybe you don't know what it's like to depend on a caregiver, but God invites you to experience this with Him.

As a product of unhealthy parenting, I may be inclined to gravitate toward unhealthy patterns, one of which is to assume my dad's ambiguity reflects God. On one hand, my dad provided for my physical needs, but on the other, he did not address my emotional ones. Was he going to leave me? Did he love me? Did he even want me? Those questions poisoned my perception of God. He felt ambiguous, too, and I wasn't sure how to move forward, or if He was even there at all. For the majority of people, relational ambiguity won't translate as imminent rejection, and even after an argument, or a season of less communication, there remains an underlying trust that the bond remains. But for others—namely, those who have experienced emotional neglect—any ambiguity within a relationship can cause significant anxiety and a fear of abandonment. "According to object relations theorists, if our childhood relationships with our primary caregivers were hallmarked by neglect, inattention, or abuse, as adults, we may expect our relationships with spouses, children, and friends to exhibit the same characteristics."[11]

Within object relations theory, you'll find *object permanence*, which describes knowing an object, or rather a person, still exists even if it's out of sight or cannot be touched or sensed in some way. Before object permanence is developed, a baby playing peekaboo believes their mom's face ceases to exist when it's hidden. As babies mature, though, they eventually understand that their mom is still there, even if they cannot see her. Because this understanding is not innately in babies, they will either grow into a healthy understanding that objects (people) are permanent even when out of view, or live in anxiety with a stunted understanding of their loved one's permanence. Interestingly enough, one of the ways to help an infant learn object permanence is to play peekaboo with them. Does God do this with us? Could the seasons we can't sense Him, due to our clouds of depression, or His own mysterious ways, serve to strengthen our understanding that He is, in fact, always there? Is this one of the ways our infinitely wise Father refines our faith? Even David seems to have felt distance with God:

> God, listen to my prayer
> and do not hide from my plea for help. (Ps. 55:1)

> LORD, why do you reject me?
> Why do you hide your face from me? (Ps. 88:14)

> How long, LORD? Will you hide forever?
> (Ps. 89:46a)

What I love about David's laments are the fact that he asked God where He was. A child who has learned through experience it's not safe to reveal their feelings to their parents probably won't have the courage to even inquire where they are.

Because "faith is the reality of what is hoped for, the proof of what is not seen" (Heb. 11:1), object permanence is a picture of faith to me. The Spirit does not require a healthy childhood in those He cultivates faith within, and oftentimes a difficult childhood increases your hunger for the hope Jesus offers, proving the gifts hidden within adversity. However, having parents who act in accordance with God's character, which entails nurturing a child's understanding of their permanence through thoughtful parenting, will naturally set their children up to transfer that relationship onto the heavenly Father. In other words, a secure attachment to parents we *can* see makes it easier to securely attach to a God we *can't* see.

The opposite is true as well. When emotionally unavailable parents cause attachment trauma through their distant way of parenting, their child's development of object permanence may be interrupted, leading to a stunted faith, and as a result, a stunted prayer life. This proves problematic since lament involves praying to a God you believe is there to hear you.

Maybe you don't struggle to believe people exist even if you don't see them, but what about their emotional bond to you? "Object constancy is the ability to feel safe in a relationship despite conflict or geographic distance. A child with strong object constancy understands that significant relationships are not damaged by time apart. A child with weak object constancy may develop irrational fears of being abandoned."[12] A healthy sense of object constancy knows that even when there has been a frustration or disappointment in the relationship, or if others fail to return texts, the distance is only temporary. A shattered object constancy, though, crafts a message to the mind that those things are a sure sign of abandonment. Death, divorce, neglect, and abuse can cause a rupture in the development of object constancy, but so can situations such as parents in the military, or parents who have little time to spend with their children. Perhaps these parents aren't abusive per se, but not being present can certainly hinder a child's ability to emotionally connect to others, including God. Feeling disconnected and alone can precede an overwhelming sense of feeling deserted.

Deserted

Some of our great Bible heroes were deserted by others, including Jesus and Paul. Paul's second letter to Timothy, his young coworker, encouraged perseverance in the face of suffering. Second Timothy was most likely written during Paul's second imprisonment in Rome, while awaiting execution. In this letter, Paul said: "At my first defense, no one stood by me, but everyone deserted me. May it not be counted against them. But the Lord stood with me and strengthened me, so that I might fully preach the word and all the Gentiles might hear it" (2 Tim. 4:16–17a). Paul was deserted, yet strengthened to continue in hope and purpose because he knew the Lord stood by him. Hebrews 13:5–6 says: "I will never leave you or abandon you. Therefore, we may boldly say, 'The Lord is my helper; I will not be afraid. What can man do to me?'" Paul experienced inner confidence that God was for him and with him, even though people had deserted him. We can know God is with us, even if our parents deserted us, but what happens in seasons when it feels like God has deserted you?

God's discipline may feel no different than a dad giving you the silent treatment, or a parent threatening to leave you. But we must remember that even when a child's behavior warrants a dad's discipline, it never warrants his desertion. There are seasons when God allows suffering in our individual stories as part of a greater story that is playing out. This story began before Eden and will continue into eternity. At times, we see through the pages of Scripture that God's people suffer through no fault of their own, but other times, their suffering is self-inflicted. And the self-inflicted suffering of one may lead to the suffering of another for no other reason than God is allowing it as a way to refine his child and further the Kingdom. As confusing and mysterious as this may be, we must remember that all of God's actions, including when He feels distant, flow from the delight he takes in the children He loves (Prov. 3:11–12).

There are two categories of discipline in Scripture, one being *instructive discipline*, and the other being *corrective discipline*. And all discipline is for the purpose of bringing His people back into right relationship with Him, never out of cruelty. "The instructive discipline of the Lord is when the Lord allows us to suffer for reasons that, whether we understand or not, he ultimately is going to use to glorify himself. The corrective discipline of the Lord is suffering the consequences of our sin."[13]

Lament is necessary in both forms of discipline. In the midst of instructive discipline, lament gives the sufferer an outlet for voicing pain and confusion at what seems like unnecessary suffering from a human standpoint. God chose to include the aching cries of the confused in His Word, both showing us the bent of the Bible toward pain, but also as an invitation to join the sorrowful, yet hopeful, cries of those who've gone before us. In seasons of corrective discipline, though, lament is more than a way of expressing pain, but also a way of confessing sin that has led to the suffering. As seen in the penitential psalms, discussed later in this book, the weary psalmist expresses sorrow for his sins and appeals to God for mercy. The penitential psalms are the humbly repentant way a believer can respond to consequences God has allowed as a way to bring them back into fellowship with Him.

Hebrews explains God's discipline this way:

> Endure hardship as discipline; God is treating you as his children. For what children are not disciplined by their father? If you are not disciplined—and everyone undergoes discipline—then you are not legitimate, not true sons and daughters at all. Moreover, we have all had human fathers who disciplined us and we respected them for it. How much more should we submit to the Father of spirits and live! (12:7–9 NIV)

While the word *discipline* was a common word that encompassed the instruction, training, and correction involved in child-rearing, here in Hebrews, there is a definite focus on the need for perseverance during discipline. Hebrews 12 goes on to compare the discipline of an earthly father to that of our heavenly Father:

> They disciplined us for a little while as they thought best; but God disciplines us for our good, in order that we may share in his holiness. No discipline seems pleasant at the time, but painful. Later on, however, it produces a harvest of righteousness and peace for those who have been trained by it. (vv. 10–11 NIV)

I do believe my dad disciplined me as he thought best, but God only disciplines us for our good so that we may share in his peace. Both instructive discipline and corrective discipline are difficult to endure, but because the Father loves his children, He intervenes as seen in the book of Lamentations.

Lamentations is not an emotional outburst, but a well-organized lament over the Babylonian siege and destruction of Jerusalem and the temple brought about by God as a result of Israel's continued rebellion. Although God disciplined His people in order to correct their rebellious behavior, it still grieved Him. As Jeremiah, commonly believed to be the author of Lamentations, said, "For no one is abandoned by the Lord forever. Though he brings grief, he also shows compassion because of the greatness of his unfailing love. For he does not enjoy hurting people or causing them sorrow" (Lam. 3:31–33 NLT). Although Lamentations is full of sorrow, there is a glimmer of hope:

> Remember my affliction and my homelessness,
> the wormwood and the poison.
> I continually remember them
> and have become depressed.
> Yet I call this to mind,
> and therefore I have hope:
>
> Because of the LORD's faithful love
> we do not perish,

for his mercies never end.
They are new every morning;
great is your faithfulness!
I say, "The Lord is my portion,
therefore I will put my hope in him."

The Lord is good to those who wait for him,
to the person who seeks him. (Lam. 3:19–25)

Lamentations is a depressing book, yet hopeful as well. It's haunting, yet healing. According to the manufactured version of God many are more comfortable worshipping, Lamentations is confrontational. Making up a more palatable version of God, though, is nothing short of idolatry. Lamentations may be uncomfortable, but it's also comforting, because we are not alone in our pain, and are reminded that no pain lasts forever. In Lamentations 3, the speaker remembered the character of God, which increased his hope even in the midst of grief and depression.

My dad's words of discipline were a whip intended to hurt, but God's discipline is a whip intended to heal. And Jesus was whipped, so we never would be in an eternal sense. "He was despised and rejected—a man of sorrows, acquainted with deepest grief" (Isa. 53:3a NLT). Jesus "was pierced for our rebellion, crushed for our sins. He was beaten so we could be whole. He was whipped so we could be healed" (v. 5 NLT). "There are seasons when the brightness of our Father's smile is eclipsed by clouds and darkness. But let us remember that God never does really forsake us. It is only a seeming forsaking with us, but in Christ's case it was a real forsaking."[14]

In Hebrew, the word for *crushed* means to be broken in pieces or shattered. Crushed may reference physical destruction, or a sense of emotional and spiritual anguish, depending on the context in which it is used in Scripture. "Scholars suggest that the crushing in Isaiah 53:5 conveys the spiritual agony the Lord Jesus experienced as the sins of the world were placed upon Him as He hung upon the cross. Far greater than the physical pain was the spiritual separation from God the Father, as the Son was abandoned to pay the price of humanity's sin."[15] Truly, no other cry in history has ever possessed the level of anguish as that of Jesus when He hung on the cross and said, "My God, my God, why have you abandoned me?" (Matt. 27:46; Mark 15:34).

His cry was borrowed from Psalm 22, an individual lament originally written by David, yet finding a fuller meaning in Christ. David's lament portrays a righteous sufferer, and there is no sufferer more righteous than Jesus. The psalmist continued by crying out: "Why are you so far from my deliverance and from my words of groaning?" (Ps. 22:1b). The Hebrew word *groaning* is a "noun depicting the roaring of a lion; roaring in distress. . . . It has the sense of a person moaning or groaning."[16] The Lamb of God may have been groaning in distress on the cross, but our Lamb will one day return as the roaring Lion of Judah. Psalm 22 began in distress; however, like lament does, it ends in the triumphant declaration: "They will come and declare his righteousness; to a people yet to be born they will declare what he has done" (v. 31). Our all-knowing King certainly knew the rest of the psalm as He groaned in pain. I suspect Jews, who were intimately familiar with the Psalms, would have heard His anguished cry from the cross and remembered the rest of Psalm 22, which ends in the hopeful reminder that the lamenting Messiah has already won the war.

But how can we know, I mean *really* know, that God won't abandon us? Stay with me, and we'll look together.

Reflection Questions

1. Do you struggle with a fear of abandonment?

2. If so, do you know what it stems from?

3. Was there a time when God felt distant? If yes, what did you do?

    Now it's your turn. Grab a journal and write your own lament. In appendix 1 you'll find words that may help you describe what you're feeling, and in appendix 2, you'll find a guide for response and prayer as you reflect on this chapter.

CHAPTER 7

Faithful Love

"Among all the arguments that can be used in pleading with God perhaps there is none stronger than this—'Have respect unto the covenant.'" [1]

CHARLES SPURGEON

Plain and simple, we need other people. Perhaps much of this book is about how others have negatively influenced my perception of God; however, the opposite has been true as well. God may have allowed the actions of others to undo me, but in His goodness, He provided faithful loved ones to help me unlearn what trauma taught me. I started yearning for the same intimacy with the Father that I was experiencing with them. And not just yearn for it, but pursue it.

The mentor who displayed maternal love toward me when I was difficult unlocked curiosity in me as to *why* she chose to stay. My friends who pursued me when I failed to respond made me wonder *why* they didn't reject me. My in-laws who continually welcomed me in as a daughter, despite not sharing my DNA, made me question *why* when they had no biological obligation. As believers, they reflected the Lord who "provides homes for those who are deserted" (Ps. 68:6), and their collective staying power began to loosen the threats of abandonment my childhood instilled in me. Their faithfulness acted as an invitation to reveal the struggling me, and not just the people-pleasing me. To my surprise, they didn't pull away, but rather, pulled me close. Would God do the same?

While it would take a combination of therapy, the faithfulness of others, and studying the Bible to understand *why* God is faithful, a peek at the past reveals that my road to understanding really began at the alter when my dad gave me to the man who would challenge all I knew to be true regarding commitment. In a magnificent church in Norman, Oklahoma, I stood before Ryan in a white gown as he vowed his devotion to me. Marriage vows honored are a beautifully tangible way to understand the steadfast love of God, and Ryan has certainly honored his to me. Ryan has been a deep well of security in my life that has expanded my experiential understanding of security within relationships more than anyone. He has stayed when my behavior would have made others run. He's weathered the days that would fall under the category of "for worse," and he has remained committed to me as sickness—more specifically, depression and PTSD—sent us home from the mission field. Without a home, car, plan, or income, that season would be under the "for poorer" promise. When we entered into the covenant of marriage before God, he vowed to love me until death parts us, and even when I failed to uphold my promises, he remained faithful to his. When we argued, he taught me healthy conflict resolution. Ryan's commitment continues to challenge my childhood, and my kinship with Ryan is how I have learned to understand God.

God's design for marriage doesn't stop at just a husband and wife, but also becomes the way a child is introduced to Him as a steadfast Father and safe haven. A child who feels unconditionally loved by parents who display faithful love to each other knows they are supported, accepted, and that even if they struggle, or misstep, they are secure in their relationship. Their plea for attention is also commonplace when its recipient is an emotionally healthy parent who is quick to offer reassurance. There have been times my kids have begged me for something, even saying, "But Mom, you promised!" They feel comfortable reminding me when I fail to honor what I have promised, also freely expressing impatience when I appear slow to act. When they persistently pursue me for something, I smile to myself and recognize that secure kids feel free to ask for what they want and need. And even as I smile, I think of how I didn't feel the same freedom in childhood, and therefore grief joins my joy, and I lament.

Perhaps despair is creeping in as you're reading this. Maybe you grew up in a broken home full of infidelity or abuse, and you've seen those patterns repeated in your own marriage. Maybe you are just now realizing how your actions may be hindering your children in understanding God's faithfulness. It's not too late. Your heartbeat is the sound of hope. But even in the journey of breaking cycles and pursuing mental, emotional, spiritual, and relational health, there will be grief when blinders are removed and you realize afresh what you didn't have as a child, and how that has shaped you as an adult. Therefore, we lament; we feel the sorrow and take it to God, but every ounce of sorrow is infused with hope when you remember that God can redeem all things.

Your insecure childhood may have led you to believe there is something inherently wrong with you, or that you only deserve love when your behavior is deemed worthy of it. But this could not be further from the truth when it comes to God. Yes, we strive to behave in a manner worthy of our calling, but it's not based on fearing abandonment, but rather on the permanence of God's promises, the permanence of our adoption. It may take time for your understanding to shift, but let me go beyond telling you that you are secure with God as His born-again child, and explain *why*.

Covenant

God is a covenant-making God, who not only creates covenants, but perfectly keeps them. In fact, the entire story of Scripture happens within the framework of covenants. One of the first things learned in Sunday school is that the Bible is made up of the Old Testament and the New Testament. Have you ever wondered, though, where we got the word *testament*? "It comes from two passages in the New Testament, one in Hebrews and one in Galatians where actually the word is properly rendered *covenant*."[2] While tradition keeps us using the word *testament*, using the term *covenant* would provide a better understanding of God's ways.

The word *covenant* may seem "church-y," irrelevant, confusing, or outdated by today's societal norms. Marriage may be one of the clearest expressions of covenantal love we have, but in a world where the need for happiness trumps vows made at the altar, it's no wonder why people choose to break covenants for the sake of their feelings. Some even may assume covenants and contracts to be synonymous; however, when examined closely, there are subtle nuances worthy of notation. You sign a contract when renting an apartment, hiring a wedding planner, or starting a new job. Both contracts and covenants are legally binding, but a covenant differs in that there is a relational component that unites the two parties in a deeply intimate way. "A covenant is a relationship between two partners who make binding promises to each other and work together to reach a common goal. They're often accompanied by oaths, signs, and ceremonies. Covenants define obligations and commitments, but they are different from a contract because they are relational and personal."[3]

The Bible is full of covenant relationships, with some being between friends or spouses, and yet others being political in nature. Most covenants, though, are established between God and man, with God as the initiator of the relationship. Understanding covenants ties together the whole story of Scripture, including the miracle of salvation. When Jesus said to His disciples, "This cup is the new covenant in my blood, which is poured out for you" (Luke 22:20), He was using covenant vocabulary and offering insight into how He fulfills each and every covenant established by God. You may be wondering why I'm talking about covenants in a book on childhood wounds and lament, but in order to understand how this relates to lament and your pursuit of intimacy with God, we must look briefly at the history of covenants within Scripture, starting at the beginning.

God created Adam and Eve, and said to them, "Be fruitful, multiply, fill the earth, and subdue it. Rule the fish of the sea, the birds of the sky, and every creature that crawls on the earth" (Gen. 1:28). God then spelled out the terms of His relationship with them, warning against eating from the tree of the knowledge of good and evil. Partaking from the tree would bring upon humanity the curse of death. The word *covenant* isn't used in Genesis 2; however, the concept is there. The Lord clearly laid out the terms of what some theologians refer to as the *covenant of works* with Adam. God didn't just request perfect obedience, or rather good works, He required it. He was clear of the consequences should they disobey, and because He is always faithful to His word, He followed through. The first humans failed their first test of covenant faithfulness, and we are still under the curse brought on by their catastrophic disobedience. In fact, if they had not sinned, there would be no childhood wounds hindering you from perfect intimacy with God. But God is faithful and the story of humanity didn't end in ashes. The rest of Scripture tells of God's beautiful, redemptive plan that is still unfolding today.

In the garden, God then addressed the serpent responsible for tempting Adam and Eve by saying: "I will put hostility between you and the woman, and between your offspring and her offspring.

He will strike your head, and you will strike his heel" (Gen. 3:15). God's words here have traditionally been understood as the "Protoevangelium," or the first gospel announcement. In a moment of everything crashing down, God cast a vision of hope by introducing the *covenant of grace*, in which we see God's unmerited favor toward men. The covenant of works required perfect obedience from man; however, the covenant of grace requires faith. All future covenants established by God are born from the covenant of grace. Within covenants, there is a covenant representative, known as the federal head, who acts on behalf of those who have been bound together through the covenant. Because this covenant head is a representative of the group, their actions are imputed onto the covenant members. The idea of federal headship is central to Paul's explanation of how death came through Adam in Romans 5, for when Adam fell, we did too.

> Now Adam is a symbol, a representation of Christ, who was yet to come. But there is a great difference between Adam's sin and God's gracious gift. For the sin of this one man, Adam, brought death to many. But even greater is God's wonderful grace and his gift of forgiveness to many through this other man, Jesus Christ. And the result of God's gracious gift is very different from the result of that one man's sin. For Adam's sin led to condemnation, but God's free gift leads to our being made right with God, even though we are guilty of many sins. For the sin of this one man, Adam, caused death to rule over many. But even greater is God's wonderful grace and his gift of righteousness, for all who receive it will live in triumph over sin and

death through this one man, Jesus Christ. (Rom. 5:14b–17 NLT)

In Jesus, every Old Testament covenant finds completion. As one who has tried, and failed, to earn a felt sense of security and love from my dad, this is comforting news. In a way, those with childhood wounds are the blessed ones who deeply yearn for, and appreciate, what the wounded, yet resurrected King has done.

While the word *covenant* may not have been present in the creation narrative, we do see it in the story of Noah: "When the LORD saw that human wickedness was widespread on the earth and that every inclination of the human mind was nothing but evil all the time, the LORD regretted that he had made man on the earth, and he was deeply grieved" (Gen. 6:5–6). God isn't aloof. He is emotionally invested in His creation, and here we see that God's heart was filled with deep grief. The word used expresses "the most intense form of human emotion, a mixture of rage and bitter anguish. Dinah's brothers felt this way after she was raped; so did Jonathan when he heard Saul planned to kill David; and David reacted similarly when he heard of Absalom's death."[4] God is unbelievably relatable in how He understands what grief feels like. He welcomes your lament not only as the Creator of emotion, but as one who laments as well. God doesn't lament because He needs something, though. He laments sin, including your parents' sinful actions to and with you. When your heart grieves what happened to you as a child, and even feels rage and bitter anguish, God grieves with you. After the flood receded, God established a covenant with Noah and his sons that He would never again wipe out the world with a flood, establishing the rainbow as a reminder of His promise. Noah is seen as a new kind of Adam, and through the "Noahic Covenant," God has committed to graciously preserve creation until the final judgment. It's through the line of Noah that the Messiah would eventually come.

Following the "Noahic Covenant," God established a covenant with Abram, called the "Abrahamic Covenant." God's redemptive plan through the history of Israel, and eventually all people, stems from this covenant. "The LORD said to Abram, 'Look from the place where you are. Look north and south, east and west, for I will give you and your offspring forever all the land that you see. I will make your offspring like the dust of the earth, so that if anyone could count the dust of the earth, then your offspring could be counted. Get up and walk around the land, through its length and width, for I will give it to you'" (Gen. 13:14b–17). Eventually, God told Abram: "'Bring me a three-year-old cow, a three-year-old female goat, a three-year-old ram, a turtledove, and a young pigeon.' So he brought all these to him, cut them in half, and laid the pieces opposite each other, but he did not cut the birds in half. Birds of prey came down on the carcasses, but Abram drove them away. As the sun was setting, a deep sleep came over Abram, and suddenly great terror and darkness descended on him" (15:9–12).

When two parties entered into a covenant, they were naturally awake to agree to the terms of the covenant, but here, while Abram is essentially passed out in a deep sleep brought upon him by God, God appears and walks alone through the bloody path between the carcasses. This speaks volumes about who God is. "When two nations joined together in a covenant, the weaker nation would walk in between animal carcasses that were cut in half. This gruesome ritual signified that if the weaker nation broke the covenant, he would bring upon himself a covenant curse, becoming like the dead animals. When God appeared to Abram, He told him to cut animals in half, but rather than telling Abram to walk through them, God Himself passed through the divided animals. This unexpected act indicated that God promised to take the curse of the covenant upon Himself if Abram broke it."[5] God knew the failure that would transpire in Abram's family, the nation of Israel. By walking alone through the animals, He was protecting Abram and his descendants from the horrific consequences of covenant failure. What a beautiful exhibition of His faithfulness, and powerful foreshadowing of Jesus, who gave us the ability to receive the blessings of the covenant through taking upon Himself the curse we deserved.

At the Last Supper, the bread broken by Jesus signified His body that would soon be broken. But it's so much deeper than that. Reminiscent of the carcasses cut in two by Abram, Jesus broke the bread. "After supper he took another cup of wine and said, 'This cup is the new covenant between God and his people—an agreement confirmed with my blood, which is poured out as a sacrifice for you'" (Luke 22:20 NLT). The new covenant is God promising to forgive the sin, and adopt those who turn their hearts toward Him. Following this, our Savior went on to walk the bloody path of crucifixion. "The purpose was that the blessing of Abraham would come to the Gentiles by Christ Jesus, so that we could receive the promised Spirit through faith" (Gal. 3:14). God established the covenant with Abraham, and then came in the form of Christ to take upon Himself the consequences of man failing to keep it. And we, regardless of ethnicity, social status, and gender, are welcomed and grafted into the family of God through Jesus; we are sons and daughters of Abraham. "For those of you who were baptized into Christ have been clothed with Christ. There is no Jew or Greek, slave or free, male and female; since you are all one in Christ Jesus. And if you belong to Christ, then you are Abraham's seed, heirs according to the promise" (vv. 27–29).

Diving into the world of covenants, while odd at first, is the very foundation of our ability to lament without fear of abandonment. Your God is the Father who will never let you go. Even when God appears slow to act, and like He has forgotten His covenant to His people through allowing suffering, we must remember that His loyal, covenantal love endures forever. Your bent toward fearing abandonment may be from well-worn pathways in your thinking paved by trauma, but there is hope for attaching to God even if you've never securely attached to a parent on earth, for everything destroyed by trauma finds restoration in Christ. And His faithful love endures forever.

Hesed

In Exodus 34, God called Moses back up to Mount Sinai, where He came down in a cloud and proclaimed both His name and character by saying:

> "The LORD—the LORD is a compassionate and gracious God, slow to anger and abounding in *faithful love* and truth, maintaining *faithful love* to a thousand generations, forgiving iniquity, rebellion, and sin. But he will not leave the guilty unpunished, bringing the consequences of the fathers' iniquity on the children and grandchildren to the third and fourth generation."
> And Moses immediately knelt low on the ground and worshiped. (vv. 6–8, emphasis mine)

The faithful love God describes Himself as abounding in is rooted in his covenant relationship with them. In Hebrew, this love is called *hesed* (sometimes transliterated as *chesed* or *khesed*). Throughout Scripture, we see *hesed* translated a multitude of ways, including mercy, goodness, unfailing love, loyal love, loving-kindness, and steadfast love, but all of these translations are an attempt to translate a Hebrew word with no perfect English equivalent. While the etymology of *hesed* remains unknown, a careful study of this concept has great implications for understanding God's faithfulness and kindness to His children. "Because of His kindness, He meets the needs of His creation by delivering them from enemies and despair (Gen. 19:19; Exod. 15:13; Ps. 109:26; Jer. 31:3)."[6] Hesed should not be misunderstood as merely a feeling, but rather love in action. Hesed intervenes for others, comes to their rescue, and indicates faithfulness to the relationship. Hesed is "the kind of love that someone demonstrates when they're keeping a promise, and when the desire to be loyal to their promise motivates them to go above and beyond and be super generous, more than what you would expect."[7] Hesed is so much more than love; it's loyal love. It's also deeper than kindness; it's a kindness that you can depend on. Love may be romanticized as nothing more than flutters in your tummy, however *hesed* is an affection that is committed no matter what. "*Hesed* describes God's mercy to sinners in offering them redemption. It proclaims His loving-kindness to save those who have made themselves enemies of God from His wrath and adopt them as His own children. *Hesed* is a loyal, enduring, steadfast love that never gives up, never abandons, and never backs out on a promise. It is the goodness of God that works in every single second of history to bring about the redemption that He promises to His people. *Hesed* is covenant love. It is a love that stays, even when it is not reciprocated."[8] One of the most tangible examples of *hesed* on earth is seen in marriage, which is further highlighted when one spouse becomes unable to care for themselves. When a wife stays and cares for her husband whose mind is slipping, and is no longer able to care for her, let alone himself, she displays *hesed*. He no longer has much to offer her, but she has promised to love him for better or for worse, in sickness and in health, and her loyalty is love in action. It's *hesed*.

Do you remember what Adam and Eve did right after they disobeyed God in the garden? They hid. They knew they had messed up, and out of shame they did all they could to conceal themselves from their Creator. But God, rich in *hesed*, immediately sought after his people. His persistent, unconditional love and mercy led Him to seek after His own even when they ran from Him. If your behavior wasn't perfect as a child, you may have hidden, both physically and emotionally, from your parents out of survival. With God, though, there is no pretending to be perfect out of survival. God loves you, knows you, and nothing you do—good or bad—can change His *hesed* toward you.

Hesed in Lament

Hesed is used all throughout Scripture in stories that you know and love.

In Isaiah 54:10, God said: "'Though the mountains move and the hills shake, my love [*hesed*] will not be removed from you and my covenant of peace will not be shaken,' says your compassionate Lord."

In Lamentations, the weeping prophet said: "Even if he causes suffering, he will show compassion according to the abundance of his faithful love [*hesed*]" (Lam. 3:32).

Micah teaches: "what it is the Lord requires of you: to act justly, to love faithfulness [*hesed*], and to walk humbly with your God" (Mic. 6:8b).

Joseph was unjustly thrown into prison, "But the Lord was with Joseph and extended kindness [*hesed*] to him. He granted him favor with the prison warden" (Gen. 39:21).

Moses praised God by saying: "With your faithful love [*hesed*], you will lead the people you have redeemed; you will guide them to your holy dwelling with your strength" (Exod. 15:13).

In Jeremiah 31, God promised to make a new covenant with Israel when He declared: "I have loved you with an everlasting love;

therefore, I have continued to extend faithful love [*hesed*] to you" (Jer. 31:3b).

And while there are some 250 times *hesed* is used in Scripture, the majority of them are in the book of Psalms, with Psalm 136 being the chief celebration of God's *hesed*. Psalm 136 begins with: "Give thanks to the LORD, for he is good. His faithful love [*hesed*] endures forever" (v. 1), and goes on to declare his enduring, faithful love twenty-five more times. When it comes to lament, the concept of God's *hesed* is integral, and through a careful study, we can see that David often appealed to God's *hesed*, like my kids do when they say, "Mom, you promised!" David chose to trust God because he was secure in God's *hesed* and understood its connection to God's faithfulness.

Psalm 6 is an individual lament where David is lamenting, and repenting, of sin. He pours out his penitent appeal based on God's faithful love, and not his own good behavior:

> Turn, LORD! Rescue me; save me because of your faithful love [*hesed*]. (v. 4)

In Psalm 25, David remembers the description of God's character from Exodus 34. David asks God to attend to him according to His merciful, faithful, good character rather than according to his sin:

> Remember, LORD, your compassion and your faithful love [*hesed*], for they have existed from antiquity. Do not remember the sins of my youth or my acts of rebellion; in keeping with your faithful love [*hesed*], remember me because of your goodness, LORD. (vv. 6–7)

Psalm 109 is an individual lament that heavily focuses on praying for his accusers to get what they deserve, but at the same time, David writes of resting in God's *hesed*:

> Let this be the LORD's payment to my accusers, to those who speak evil against me. But you, LORD, my Lord, deal kindly with me for your name's sake; because your faithful love [*hesed*] is good, rescue me. (vv. 20–21)

And David knows that God's hesed is better than anything this life has to offer:

> My lips will glorify you because your faithful love [*hesed*] is better than life. (Ps. 63:3)

God is committed to you, and His commitment is not founded on your goodness, but rather on His ability to keep being God. Your parents may have abandoned you, or even just threatened to do so, but God will do neither. Lament the wounds that have made you doubt God's faithful love, lament the pain that lingers still, and remember the covenant promises that have been given to you through Christ.

Reflection Questions

1. How familiar were you with biblical covenants prior to this chapter?

2. Define *hesed* in your own words.

3. How will understanding God's hesed calm your fear of abandonment?

Now it's your turn. Grab a journal and write your own lament. In appendix 1 you'll find words that may help you describe what you're feeling, and in appendix 2, you'll find a guide for response and prayer as you reflect on this chapter.

CHAPTER 8

Breaking the Cycle

*"Oh, that you would choose life, so that you
and your descendants might live!"*

DEUTERONOMY 30:19b NLT

My youngest climbed in my bed to snuggle one evening, but being tired, I checked out and laid on my side. I had *turned away* from him. He asked me to *turn toward* him, but I was so comfortable and distracted, that I made up some excuse as to why I couldn't. At the sound of his disappointed "Okay," perspective reminded me just how fleeting these days are that my son will want to curl up next to me with his nose against mine. I pushed aside weariness, set my phone down, and *turned toward* my son. His big, contented sigh sung of all being right in his world. As he drew close, his warm breath married mine, and although I didn't understand just yet, the sweet sound of secure attachment echoed in each sleepy exhale.

I woke up the next day, and made my way to my weekly therapy session, where I nonchalantly mentioned that just the night before, I chose to put my phone down and *turn toward* my son. I saw no significance other than I was a mom remembering to savor childhood. Switching gears, I started telling her that I was working on this very chapter about breaking family patterns. She smiled and asked me to elaborate. While you may not find the term *cycle-breaker* in a psychology textbook, you may have seen it while scrolling social media. "A *cycle-breaker* is somebody who sees an unhealthy cycle of behavior in their family of origin (meaning the family they grew up in) and intentionally works to break that cycle."[1] This topic came up often in our sessions because, like most people, I didn't just instinctively know how to parent differently than I was parented. Well, maybe some people know how, but typically it's easier to challenge well-worn patterns, carved in a family tree, with professional help. For me, I had to learn what cycle I was stuck in before I could learn to break it.

After hearing that I had chosen to turn toward my son, my therapist commended me for doing the opposite of what I experienced as a child. She understood that "It is in the small moments, when we feel the other person fully present, fully engaged, connected and accepting, that we make the most powerful, enduring bonds."[2] When you hear the term *emotional neglect*, obvious cases, easily identified as neglectful, may come to mind. What's interesting, though, and honestly startling in this digital age, is that emotional neglect can be quite subtle, yet damaging, nonetheless. "A parent may truly love his child, but if he is sitting at a computer posting on social media about how much he loves his child while the infant is in another room, awake, hungry, and crying, the infant experiences no love. To the infant, skin-to-skin warmth, the smell of the parent, the sights and sounds of her caregivers, the attentive and responsive caregiver's actions—that becomes *love*."[3] And when a child asks for a gesture of love, and a parent ignores it, or flat-out refuses—that becomes the opposite of love. In an individual lament, David turned his heart to God, and asked God to *turn toward* him. I believe he was confident that God would respond to his distress: "Answer me, Lord, for your faithful love is good. In keeping with your abundant compassion, *turn to me*. Don't hide your face from your servant, for I am in distress. Answer me quickly!" (Ps. 69:16–17, emphasis mine).

There was great significance in that moment of *turning toward* my son, and giving him my attention. "The thousands of these loving, responsive interactions shape the developing brain of the infant. These loving moments literally build the foundation of the organizing brain."[4] My son was no longer an infant, but I have to believe that our seemingly insignificant moment was working toward him growing into a man who knows he is loved, and therefore, knows how to love others, God included. I pray he follows Jesus every day of his life, and laments when grief is woven into his story. My hope is that as he learns emotional intimacy with me that will translate to intimacy with God.

I cannot stress enough how difficult it can be to recognize gaping wounds from childhood emotional neglect, because it's not about something harmful given, but rather something good withheld. And it doesn't have to be everything good, or even from both parents. "Another kind of neglect—"splinter" neglect—occurs when many aspects of development are normal and some key systems receive appropriately timed experiences, but one or more does not—leading to the absence of a critical aspect of healthy development."[5] This can have devastating consequences, and produce adults who don't understand why they act and feel a certain way. And by act, I mean in an emotionally immature way that wreaks havoc on those they do life with, when unbeknownst to them, a childhood wound has been irritated and their wounded inner child has taken the reigns. This type of neglect may not be recognized as the source of emotional and relational difficulty in adulthood due to certain aspects of their upbringing being healthy. And you can't break a cycle you don't realize you're in. Portions of my upbringing were healthy, as my mom was nurturing and as available as cancer allowed, and my dad provided for my basic needs. Therefore,

I didn't understand there was a cycle to break because I grew up unaware of just how damaging his lack of emotional connectedness was on my self-esteem, my ability to connect with others, my perceived lovability, and my willingness to turn to God in transparency and dependency. A parent and child weren't designed to simply coexist under the same roof. A father is meant to be the refuge his child seeks safety within, and the springboard from which the child is launched into a securely attached relationship with the Lord.

Childhood wounds are not a death sentence when it comes to being a loving parent yourself, and they are not a hopeless thorn in the flesh that make intimacy with God a fruitless pursuit. But childhood wounds ignored oftentimes wound the next generation. And the wounds I had obtained as a daughter were not only infecting my relationship with my children, but were laying the foundation for their future as parents. The first step in healing is recognizing the wound is even there. Failure to do so is like putting a Band-Aid on a gunshot wound when what you need is intense wound care. "Wound care involves every stage of wound management. This includes diagnosing wound type, considering factors that affect wound healing, and the proper treatments for wound management. Once the wound is diagnosed and all factors are considered, the treatment facility can determine the best treatment options. Depending on the wound severity, you may need more care and attention for your wound."[6] Although wound care may be for physical wounds, this concept easily applies to the invisible wounds of the soul. If we are going to be a people who intimately connect with God, we must be people willing to start at the moment of wounding and look at how that wound is hindering our relationship with Him. Wounds that have healed can still leave scars, or numbness, or even a limp like Jacob walked with after having his hip dislocated (Gen. 32:25). Emotional wounding is no different. Like a child adopted by a wonderful family may still struggle with feeling abandoned, you can be saved, and yet still be bent toward your wounded childhood ways. This figurative limp, though, doesn't mean you can't live in intimacy with God. And just like God uses our weakness to show His power, your emotional limp testifies to what God has saved you from. Over time, my limp has become the precious evidence of the humility I've gained through heartache, which is of utmost importance in the life of a lamenter who looks to her Father and says, "Help."

Cycle-Breaking Is a Choice

During therapy, our conversation organically flowed to focusing on the differences between my dad's choices, particularly his choice to die, and my choice to live. My celebration was cut short, though, as shame seeped into the room like the invisible killer, carbon monoxide. I figuratively drifted to sleep and became hyperfocused on the days I was convinced I was a burden on my family, and eventually, like my dad, believed death to be the solution. One aspect of being a cycle-breaker, for me, has been learning to celebrate my strides toward life, even when shame reminds me of my past steps toward death. In order to do this, though, I had to understand my relationship with shame.

Shame, while destructive, tried to manage me from a place of wanting to protect me. When Adam and Eve sinned in the garden, their first instinct was to hide out of shame. I love that God pursued them still. Hiding physically, though, doesn't silence the internal shaming heard in your own inner dialogue. You may think, "I messed up," but before long, you tell yourself, "I'm a bad mom." This is what shame does. It takes something you've done, or had done to you, and tells you that because of those things, now you are bad. This shaming part of you is not speaking truth, but like bottling up any emotion, suppressing it will not subdue it. Acknowledging it, and understanding it with compassion, will. And one of the ways to do this is by understanding that oftentimes your shame part stems from wounding in childhood. If you spilled milk as a child, and your parent shamed you for it, shame then began working to manage your behavior so you wouldn't be seen as a bad child. Shame was attempting to protect you. And really, their shaming voice became your inner voice. Once that child becomes an adult, shame may manage them through perfectionistic behavior that believes it must earn approval from others, God included, through ideal behavior. In other words, "If I am good, I am loved and accepted." In that counseling office, as I began comparing myself to my dad, I was overwhelmed by shame and consumed by thoughts of what a bad mom I was for the decades I danced with death. As my therapist helped me welcome shame, acknowledge it, and remind myself why it keeps showing up, the burden lifted. That part of me realized it wasn't needed in the same way that it was when I was a child. Clarity created compassion for the younger parts within me, but also courage to face the future and break the cycle.

Clarity gave me hope, but also a complicated companion named grief.

> Grief over losing my dad to suicide.

> *O Lord, why didn't you stop my dad's suicide? Please relieve my pain. But even as I wait, I trust You, and am thankful to be Your daughter.*

> Grief over the years I nearly copied him.

> *O Lord, why did You let me get so close to leaving my family? Thank You for opening my eyes and filling my darkness with Your light. Thank You for giving me joy in motherhood. "For you, LORD, rescued me from death, my eyes from*

tears, my feet from stumbling. I will walk before the LORD *in the land of the living" (Ps. 116:8–9).*

Grief that my children live knowing the hard parts of my story.

Lord, why? Losing their grandpa to suicide was already hard, but now they live knowing how I struggled so deeply. Help them to see Your healing power in my life, and use it to create compassion in them for those who feel hopeless. I trust You to take care of them and use their stories for Your glory.

Grief over the pain of cycle-breaking.

God, why did You let this be my story? Give me strength and wisdom as I do this hard, inner work. Help the generations following me turn to You as their Lord. This is hard, but I love and trust You. My family is worth it. You are worth it.

And as I am learning to run in healing, grief over the loss of my old coping mechanism.

O Lord, how long will I feel torment over how I have coped all these years in unhealthy ways? How long will I feel shame? Help me to remember there is no condemnation as Your child. Please help me to continue choosing godly ways to grieve and cope. I trust You, for You are my life, "my rock and my Redeemer" (Ps. 19:14).

When suicidal ideation has been your automatic coping mechanism for decades, as in the way you've endured by remembering you always have a way to escape, the loss of those suicidal thoughts and plans can induce grief. Some may judge grief in this scenario as sinful, but grief is felt when you lose anything you once held dear. Breaking up with any destructive habit can feel like divorcing someone you dearly loved and depended on. As a believer, no grip of death can overpower the hope that is mine through Christ, but I'm human and I live in a fallen body that gets sick and can fall victim to deception. Through Christ, sin has no dominion over me, but my flesh is still bent toward it, "For those who live according to the flesh have their minds set on the things of the flesh, but those who live according to the Spirit have their minds set on the things of the Spirit. Now the mindset of the flesh is death, but the mindset of the Spirit is life and peace" (Rom. 8:5–6). I am not in the flesh, but rather, in the Spirit. And because of this, I am able to choose life. I was once blind, but now I see. Along with new sight, though, has been letting go of, or rather fleeing from, the Enemy's plan for my life—for your life—which is death. Death of my faith, death of my relationship with God, death of my prayer life (including lament), death of my witness, death of my fruitfulness, death of my joy, and death of my hope. As a believer, I'm convinced that even if I had succumbed to suicide, I would have been in the joyful presence of God upon waking in eternity. But what if my death had increased the chances of my children or grandchildren copying me? And what if they weren't yet believers? Then the Enemy taking me out, even just on earth, would have had eternal consequences for my ancestors. We are more than conquerors through Christ (Rom. 8:37), and learning how to walk in victory has included learning to break the cycle of my childhood so that as I run in freedom (or, possibly, limp in freedom), my children are inclined to as well.

    As my hour with my therapist drew to an end, she mentioned hearing a song on life and death, and while I intently listened to her, the Spirit was moving deep within me. I could not stop thinking these three words: "*Deuteronomy, life, death.*" I tried to ignore them and pay attention to her, but the Spirit's leading to go to Scripture was strong and steady. I blurted out that there was something I needed to look up in the Bible. As a woman of faith herself, she followed my lead and encouraged me to read it aloud. I turned to Deuteronomy 30 (ESV).

"Moses charged the Israelites to listen to the Lord and obey. No matter what the Israelites encountered in the promised land, they were to keep in mind that they were to choose to obey. The final responsibility always rests with the people. They not only had to choose, but the only right choice was obedience. There were no options."[7] As I opened up my Bible app, and I saw the section title—"The Choice of Life and Death"—something in my heart softened and immediately knew I was being reminded there was no middle ground regarding my affections, desires, contemplations, and plans.

Moses continued: "The LORD your God will delight in you if you obey his voice and keep the commands and decrees written in this Book of Instruction, and if you *turn to* the LORD your God with all your heart and soul" (Deut. 30:10 NLT, emphasis mine). *Turn to.* It leapt off the screen, and with a gasp, I said to my therapist, "That's what lament is! A *turning toward* God." It was beginning to make sense.

I kept reading: "For this commandment that I command you today is not too hard for you, neither is it far off" (v. 11 ESV). Moses was right in that if we are called by God to obey, we are empowered to understand what is being asked, and to follow through. The Holy Spirit brings to remembrance the commands of the Lord, but He also gives us the power to choose to obey them. God was showing me that I did, in fact, understand what He was asking of me, and I did have the capacity to make the right choice.

Moses continued:

"See, I have set before you today life and good, death and evil. If you obey the commandments of the LORD your God that I command you today, by loving the LORD your God, by walking in his ways, and by keeping his commandments and his statutes and his rules, then you shall live and multiply, and the LORD your God will bless you in the land that you are entering to take possession of it. But if your heart *turns away*, and you will not hear, but are drawn away to worship other gods and serve them, I declare to you today, that you shall surely perish. You shall not live long in the land that you are going over the Jordan to enter and possess. I call heaven and earth to witness against you today, that I have set before you life and death, blessing and curse. Therefore choose life, that you and your offspring may live, loving the LORD your God, obeying his voice and holding fast to him, for he is your life and length of days . . ." (vv. 15–20a ESV, emphasis mine)

This story may have been originally about the Israelites who were nearing the promised land, but the wider application felt personal. I, too, was entering and taking possession of new territory. Every day, the choice between life and death is before me—before *us*. Choosing life, yet remaining focused on death as a way to cope through life, is really just choosing death in disguise, for a focus on death *turns you away* from the Lord. Choosing life not only blesses me, but those after me. Choosing death, however, becomes like a curse on the generations after me. I know, because years later, I am still having to explain my dad's death to his grandchildren. Moses warned the Israelites of being drawn away to worship other gods and serve them, and I sensed the Spirit warning me against being drawn away to worship other gods—namely, suicide—and serving its purpose. Trusting suicide as a savior from pain is exactly that—trusting a false god. In the words of David, "Turn away from evil and do what is good" (Ps. 34:14), and what is good is choosing life and single-minded devotion to the one true God. The lives of our offspring depend upon which choice we make.

As I read the Word, and processed the applications aloud, my eyes welled up with tears, as did my therapist's. The Lord was with us—in us, in our relationship, in what she was teaching me, in the not-so-random song about life and death she had just heard—just all of it. Before I left, my therapist smiled and pointed out the beautiful connection in my *turning toward* God and my *turning toward* my son. What I did for my son was attachment behavior that nurtured secure, emotional, safety between us—it was breaking the cycle. "When a person has identified their family's patterns, processed the impact, and begun to heal those wounds, they can start to look at how to break that family cycle."[8] And this often happens through thousands of mundane moments that cumulatively break bondage. Choosing life, but also lamenting as I do the hard work of making that choice, has increased my capacity to choose emotional intimacy with my children over being controlled by my childhood.

God deserves the glory for opening my eyes to all of this; however, one of the ways He has done this is through therapy. "It's interesting—most people think about therapy as something that involves going in and undoing what happened. But whatever your past experiences created in your brain, the associations exist and you can't just delete them. You can't get rid of the past. Therapy is more about building *new* associations, making new, healthier default pathways. It is almost as if therapy is taking your two-lane dirt road and building a four-lane freeway alongside it. The old road stays, but you don't use it much anymore. Therapy is building a better alternative, a new default."⁹ As I continue mothering in a life-giving, cycle-breaking way, I praise God for the new associations He has built, and how they are becoming my new default.

Cycle-Breaking Has Purpose

Sometimes you don't know what you didn't have as a child until you're challenged to be that very thing to your own child. And because your body remembers what you've been through, the simplest and most endearing moment with your baby can trigger a trauma response that you never saw coming.

The daughter who tells me her deepest secret shines a light on the secrets I never felt safe to share.

The son who tells me his hopes and dreams highlights those I didn't feel safe enough to disclose.

Hearing them talk of breakups transports me back to crying after my first breakup in the basement, only to walk upstairs and pretend like nothing had just happened. I never expected raising children to introduce me to my inner child still in need of raising. You see, as you break cycles, you inadvertently break the chains that have trapped parts of you in childhood. Each milestone with my children becomes a new key that unlocks grief, but also a new opportunity to grow in maturity and nearness to God.

I've grown immensely; however, anticipatory grief reminds me that there are more moments to come. I suspect gathering with women and watching my daughters try on wedding dresses will invite grief into the joyous occasion as I remember standing alone in the dressing room in my gown. Watching my daughter hold her first child will remind me of giving birth without my mom. As my son smiles at his bride walking down the aisle, my joy will taste grief as I remember my mom's empty chair at my wedding. As I delight in my future grandchildren, there will be grief that my dad's death killed his chance to know his. But this is the hopeful sorrow of being a cycle-breaker. Confronting the pain may feel like an insurmountable obstacle, but you can either confront it yourself, or allow it to confront you. One way is by choice and can feel empowering, the other will most likely feel like a hijacking that is going to end in an emotional crash. Confronting the pain opens the path to healing, but also to finding purpose within the pain, which I learned one day in the grocery store.

I walked into Trader Joe's and noticed their typical wall of blooms had multiplied out the door to a flower market set up just for Mother's Day. What began as a quick trip to grab a slice of my husband's favorite Chantilly Cream Vanilla Bean Cake, was unexpectedly interrupted like trauma tends to do. I couldn't help but wonder, "Were they buying them for their moms?" I felt like I didn't belong. My husband and children always celebrate me, but Mother's Day goes both ways. You're celebrated by your kids, but in a perfect world, you're the grown-up kid doing the celebrating. I walked over to the flowers and considered buying some. I figured if I could blend in, then no one would know the storm raging in my soul. I noticed purple hyacinths, which my mother loved. I considered buying some in honor of her, but as I approached them, something in me couldn't even touch them. I could not get out of there fast enough.

This is trauma. This is flight.

Sometimes the most unsuspecting moment can activate a response in you, and while I was caught off guard in Trader Joe's, I had learned enough to recognize what was happening. But even so, my body still responded; grief still overwhelmed me, images of her death still blindsided me, and thoughts of my dad ensued. I grabbed the cake and left. As I drove home, I felt the gentle tug in my heart to *turn toward* God in my complicated grief, for if I ignored my grief and *turned away* from God, surely my kids would get the brunt of my emotional storm.

Lord, I'm so sad. Why did You take my mom? It's been decades and still hurts so much. Will it ever stop hurting; will I ever stop imagining her death? Help me to love my kids and not let grief steal my ability to break the cycle. Thank You that my sadness won't last forever and one day I will be with You in perfect joy.

I lamented, sighed as I felt hope remind my grief of the coming joy, and then stopped by Target on my way home. When I walked by the aisle of Mother's Day cards, I stood in front of the section while others around me picked out their cards and went on their way. I felt like I had no business being there, almost like my membership was cancelled to anything involving mothers. Everyone was shopping; I was frozen.

Again, a trauma response.

That's the thing about grief. It never goes away. It may shift over time, but when you least expect it, *whoosh*, you're flooded. There's hope, but there is also pain, and hopeful grief is still grief. It's healthy to acknowledge the dichotomy of hope and grief in the life of a believer, for acknowledgment precedes lamenting it.

The next morning I felt somber, with feelings reminiscent of when I prepared to attend my mother's funeral. Except I wasn't going to a funeral, but rather a Mother's Day Tea at a local elementary school. The school proactively presented an opportunity for women in the community to attend as a "stand-in mom" for children who either didn't have a mother or whose mother couldn't attend. I put on a dress, curled my hair, and tried to look nice as a way to communicate to the child I would sit with that they were special.

The school counselor paired me with an eight-year-old girl whose red, teary eyes articulated what she couldn't. My heart broke, but with the breaking came compassion and courage to be for her what I have needed. I have been her, and still am in many ways. Showing up for her was also working to heal the little girl within me. We sat together, mostly in silence on her end, as she halfway *turned away* from me. Eventually I said her name, followed by, "I don't have a mom, either." Despite her grief, her countenance changed, and she finally *turned toward* me. In a sea of happy children with their mothers, I believe she was getting a taste of secure attachment. I saw her and she felt known. As the two of us felt camaraderie within our sadness, I saw purpose in my grief. As her little hand held fast to mine, I prayed that someday she will *turn toward* God and hold fast to Him.

There is grief, but also God's glory within it when it's acknowledged, lamented, accepted, and then lived out with purpose.

Reflection Questions

1. Why do you think unhealthy patterns are often repeated?

2. Are there ways you have broken cycles in your life?

3. Explain how lament plays a role in breaking unhealthy family patterns.

Now it's your turn. Grab a journal and write your own lament. In appendix 1 you'll find words that may help you describe what you're feeling, and in appendix 2, you'll find a guide for response and prayer as you reflect on this chapter.

CHAPTER 9

Penitential Lament

*"Let me learn by paradox that the way down is the way up,
that to be low is to be high, that the broken heart is the
healed heart, that the contrite spirit is the rejoicing spirit,
that the repenting soul is the victorious soul."*[1]

THE VALLEY OF VISION

"How many times a day do you think about suicide?" the psychiatrist asked me in the early days of finally getting help. Having lost count of these automatic thoughts, I froze in fear that my concealment would lead to another hospitalization. I wasn't trying to lie; I really didn't know. My thoughts were bent toward overgeneralized thinking, a distorted thought pattern birthed in the dark pits of despair, where hope is the enemy. While antithetical to the gospel, I thought it would always feel hopeless, and life would *never* get better.

With suicide being my key to unlock eternity, it not only grew more attractive each day, but it felt attainable through my dad's completion of it. The choosing of death, which would have been the most devastating mistake of my life, is a hellish scheme from antiquity, offered to me as a coping skill that I grew to secretly cherish. I loved what suicide promised, and protected my plans so no one would take them from me. The progression from intrusive thoughts out of my control, to thoughts I sought out, to commands I listened to, to plans I refused to let go of, could have been taken to God at any point. However, my pride foolishly implored me to take matters from the hands pierced to give me life into my own hands readied for murder. But there is no place for murder, or thoughts of murder, in a child of God. Regarding the devil, Jesus said: "He was a murderer from the beginning and does not stand in the truth, because there is no truth in him. When he tells a lie, he speaks from his own nature, because he is a liar and the father of lies (John 8:44).

I was a daughter of God whose thoughts spoke from the devil's nature. That's a sickening realization I've had to grieve and lament. Looking back at those decades before I received professional help, my initial thought may not have been sinful, but I have grown to believe that I do possess power in what I do with that thought once it intrudes my mind. And when I welcomed a thought, devised a plan, and cherished my iniquity as a savior of sorts, what was an unfortunate symptom of my diagnosed illness and trauma crossed the line into sin.

And why do I share this in a book focused on lament? Because no one laments what they refuse to surrender. Before I learned to lament my sin, I had to see my sin—namely, suicide—for what it was. "Every sin, every wrongdoing, no matter what kind—whether acted out in behavior or nurtured secretly in some dark place of our heart (Matt. 5:28)—is a manifestation of something we *believe*. Every sin is born out of a belief that disobeying God (wrongdoing) will produce a happier outcome than obeying God (right-doing)."[2] Sin begins with desire, and mine was for joy. Jesus endured pain for the joy set before Him (Heb. 12:2); I wanted to end pain to hasten the joy set before me. I was being controlled by a satanic promise that used my desire to deceive me. And deception leads to disobedience, which leads to death.

Recognizing Sinful Patterns

John's account of Jesus's interaction with the woman at the well includes Jesus asking her about her husband, to which the woman revealed that she had no husband. "Jesus said to her, 'You are right in saying, "I have no husband"; for you have had five husbands, and the one you have now is not your husband'" (John 4:17–18a ESV). Jesus wasn't just pointing out her sin, but also her sin *pattern*. The Spirit convicted me of my sinful plans to end it all, but it was by way of my therapist that He helped me understand why I was stuck in that thought pattern. My therapist didn't just point out the problem with suicide, she helped me dig down to the root of it. If you don't get down to the root of weeds, it's amazing how fast they grow back. My therapist understood this, and so with great sensitivity, she helped me open the closed door of my soul, and helped me engage my inner child I had avoided my whole life.

Underneath my polished exterior were younger parts of me that had been deeply wounded in childhood. While no one saw these parts that were exiled deep within me, my behavior revealed them. Exiled parts are often the parts of us that, after experiencing trauma, have become burdened by various emotions and essentially frozen in time. These parts hold emotions such as shame, fear, and hurt from experiences early in life. For instance, if you were yelled at for crying when you were young, then you may have a part today that feels shame if you cry around others. In order to function as a good wife, loving mom, devoted follower of Christ, faithful friend, dedicated church member, and productive member of society, the pain from childhood had to be pushed away. Out of sight, out of mind, right? However, "Powerful feelings of fear, failure, loneliness, rage, and shame cannot be suppressed altogether. What those feelings really need is to be listened to, fully gotten, and soothed. If they are not tended to, they eventually show up as flashbacks, panic attacks, depression, relationship difficulties, or chronic illness."[3]

To maintain the exile of these burdened younger parts longing to be seen and heard, we have both "managers" (protective and proactive parts) and "firefighters" (protective and reactive parts). Managers are focused on keeping you safe and operating successfully. "Most people like their managers a great deal, because they get things done, they look good to others, and they often get lots of approval from the outside world for achievements, high standards, and caretaking of others."[4] For example, exiled inside of me was a young, anxious part birthed from my dad's controlling, critical behavior. As I grew up, his critical voice became my critical, inner voice. To a degree, an inner critic may prove helpful in shielding you from pain by leading you to recognize and correct a mistake. However, when an inner critic manifests in an extreme way, the destruction does not outweigh its short-term motivational benefits. As an adult, I didn't need my inner critic like I did as a child, and in realizing that, I saw it needed to be understood in order to be transformed. Understanding her meant looking at the ways she showed up with curiosity.

Initially, you may label your inner critic as bad and something to be pushed away. But I would love for you to embrace compassion with me for a moment. There is a reason this managing part of you exists. Children who hurt, yet lack the ability to articulate their need for love, oftentimes act out. While yelling at the child to correct their behavior may modify their actions in the moment, it won't raise them to be emotionally healthy adults in the long run. At one time, you needed your inner critic to help you survive in childhood by motivating you to be perfect so no one would criticize or hurt you. Perfectionism is one of the classic ways my inner critic tried to protect me. If I was overly criticized as a child, that wounded part of me would be exiled, and perfectionism would step in to manage the pain by eliciting perfect behavior from me. However, below the inner critic is an anxious child who needs to know they are loved for who they are, not for their perfect behavior.

Perfectionism, while unattainable and unhealthy, was doing its best to help me—to proactively protect me from feeling the pain of childhood. It had constructed a fortress inside of me, attempting to control my chaos. But what happens when a situation is so triggering that a manager can no longer protect you? This is where "firefighters" (protective and reactive parts) swoop in to save the day. When your anxiety reaches a dangerous level, a firefighter attempts to protect you by frantically reacting to the emergency. Firefighters serve as a distraction for the mind when the once-managed pain breaks free. Your firefighter may be obsessively shopping, alcohol, or prescription drugs, but whatever it is, the firefighters jumps into action without considering the consequences. Some firefighters are sinful, but some aren't in and of themselves. For example, moving your body is healthy, but when something gets unbalanced and exercise, which can glorify God, becomes your savior, it's sinful. It's idolatry.

Suicidal thoughts were my primary firefighter, and unfortunately, they did not consider the consequences. They told me that if the pain got to be too much, I could stop it. Counting on suicidal thoughts to save you is essentially playing with fire, as other Christians have succumbed to suicide in a moment of crisis. No vocation is immune to suicide, for sadly, even pastors have been hijacked in a moment of overwhelming distress. If sin, or thoughts of sin, helps put out your inner fire, it is never a quick fix and will only prolong and intensify the pain. Buried inside of me was an anxious little girl in need of nurturing. Maybe my parents weren't able to nurture me to the degree I needed, but I learned that I could nurture, and essentially raise, the little parts of me that were frozen in childhood. Through therapy, I was given the tools to recognize the firefighters, managers, and the exiled parts of me that needed to be seen. I also learned that as I nurtured my inner parts, I didn't need the unhealthy ways of coping I used to depend on.

Learning the *why* behind my dependency on suicide was important; however, the responsibility still fell on me regarding what I would do with the information. Both the seriousness of sin, and the importance of action on our part, were illustrated by Jesus when He said, "If your eye causes you to stumble, gouge it out and throw it away. It is better for you to enter life with one eye than to have two eyes and be thrown into the fire of hell" (Matt. 18:9 NIV). We cannot ignore sinful patterns that stem from our youngest days. God already knows every sinful bent of your heart and mind, and while horrific abuse done to you as a child may be the reason that bent is there, our responsibility remains. Therapy may have been helpful in helping me recognize my brokenness, but it was Scripture that helped me rightly handle it. And if not rightly handled, your newly recognized patterns can become that which your mind, and the Enemy, use to condemn you, turning your gaze from God back to the sin that controls you. We only have two options with sin: allow it to *turn us away* from the Father in shame, or *turn us toward* the Father in surrender. I believe we see this theme in the story of Judas Iscariot, who famously let remorse over his sin turn him from God rather than to Him.

And remember what lament is, a *turning*.

Choosing to Turn Away

Judas Iscariot was among the twelve apostles of Jesus. Matthew's gospel says, "Judas Iscariot, went to the chief priests and said, 'What are you willing to give me if I hand him over to you?' So they weighed out thirty pieces of silver for him. And from that time he started looking for a good opportunity to betray him" (Matt.

26:14–16). Even though Judas was a disciple, he sought out the right moment to betray Jesus. As the story progresses, we see the first Lord's Supper, followed by Peter's infamous denial, and finally Jesus admit to his disciples, "I am deeply grieved to the point of death. Remain here and stay awake with me" (v. 38). Jesus went a little farther before He finally fell with His face toward the ground, but His heart toward His father. He lamented: "My Father, if it is possible, let this cup pass from me. Yet not as I will, but as you will" (v. 39). While Jesus was still in the garden, Judas arrived. "A large mob with swords and clubs was with him from the chief priests and elders of the people. His betrayer had given them a sign: 'The one I kiss, he's the one; arrest him.' So immediately he went up to Jesus and said, 'Greetings, Rabbi!' and kissed him" (vv. 47–49). With that fateful kiss, Jesus was taken, arrested, and led away. "Then Judas, his betrayer, seeing that Jesus had been condemned, was full of remorse and returned the thirty pieces of silver to the chief priests and elders. 'I have sinned by betraying innocent blood,' he said" (27:3–4a). Yes, Judas felt remorse, and he regretted betraying Jesus, but rather than turning to God, lamenting his actions with a repentant change of heart, Judas wished his actions could simply be undone. And speaking of his remorse, other versions state that Judas *changed his mind*. The Greek word for "changed" in this verse is *metamélomai*. "Metamélomai, on the part of man, means little or nothing more than a selfish dread of the consequence of what one has done, whereas metanoéō means regret and forsaking the evil by a change of heart brought about by God's Spirit."[5] We see metanoéō in Acts 2:38 when Peter encouraged others to repent by saying, "Repent and be baptized, each of you, in the name of Jesus Christ for the forgiveness of your sins, and you will receive the gift of the Holy Spirit."

Upon realizing his sinful actions, Judas "threw the silver into the temple and departed. Then he went and hanged himself"

(Matt. 27:5). Turning from God in remorse was a segue to suicide, whereas turning toward God in confession is always the pathway to life. Maybe suicide is not your struggle, but what about bitterness? Jealousy? Sexual immorality? All of it leads to death. The head religious leaders took the blood money Judas had earned through his betrayal and "talked about what to do with the money. Then they decided to buy land to bury strangers in. Because of this, that land is called the Field of Blood to this day" (vv. 7–8 NLV). Judas, whose love of money was suicide, ironically bought his own graveyard.

While the story of Judas is tragic, he is not the only example given to us of how to respond in the face of recognizing the horror of our actions. There is a better way; there is lament.

Choosing to Turn Toward

The Psalms contain many songs of lament that offer timely examples of how to cry out to God in sorrow from a place of hope, but did you know that seven of the laments, known as the "penitential psalms," are specifically designed to lament both personal and communal sin? These psalms, traditionally Psalms 6, 32, 38, 51, 102, 130, and 143, offer us a model to follow and vocabulary to adopt as our own.

Psalm 51, one of the most well-known penitential psalms, is titled "Create in Me a Clean Heart, O God" (ESV). "David composed this psalm as a result of Nathan the prophet convicting him of his sins, both in his committing adultery with Bathsheba and in his arranging for the murder of Bathsheba's husband, Uriah the Hittite" (2 Sam. 12:1–14).[6] Nestled in the middle of this singer's cry for forgiveness, he said: "The sacrifices of God are a broken spirit; a broken and contrite heart, O God, you will not despise" (v. 17 ESV). God loves contrition as it shines with humility, and we know from Scripture that because "God opposes the proud but gives grace to the humble" (James 4:6 ESV), He will give you the grace to turn to Him and confess your sin.

As I worked with my therapist regarding my behavior and thought patterns, the Spirit was simultaneously transforming me through the renewing of my mind. God was maturing my faith by opening my eyes to the seriousness of the sin I was secretly holding dear, and showing me how to move forward through Scripture. Our thoughts matter, and God sees every single one of them, including the sinful ones we don't even want to admit to ourselves.

While trauma, and perhaps even the makeup of my brain, certainly add difficulty, the responsibility to fight sin always falls on me. Subscribing to the worldly way of thinking that trauma, or a diagnosis, nullifies your obligation to pursue holiness completely denies the power of Christ living in and through you. In that same vein, James instructs us to: "Submit yourselves therefore to God. Resist the devil, and he will flee from you. Draw near to God, and he will draw near to you. Cleanse your hands, you sinners, and purify your hearts, you double-minded. Be wretched and mourn and weep. Let your laughter be turned to mourning and your joy to gloom. Humble yourselves before the Lord, and he will exalt you" (James 4:7–10 ESV). James's use of laughter speaks to just how casually the recipients of his message were treating the sin in their lives. And all these years later, are we any different? James echoes Paul, who cried out in response to his sin, "What a wretched man I am!" (Rom. 7:24), by his instruction to be wretched and mourn and weep. This is exactly where the gift of David's penitential words come in as a model for us to follow in lamenting our own sin.

In God's children who fail to mourn over their continued sin, you'll find a prideful heart quick to ignore the Spirit's leading to confess that which is abhorrent to the Lord. A broken and contrite heart comes to the Lord in confession, admitting that which has entangled it. Charles Spurgeon explains the beauty of a broken and contrite heart this way:

> A broken spirit signifies that now *all the secrets and essences of the spirit have flowed out.* You remember what happened when that holy woman broke the alabaster box; we read that "the house was filled with the odour of the ointment." A broken heart cannot keep secrets. Now is all revealed, now its essence goes forth. Far too much of our praying, and of our worship, is like closed-up boxes; you cannot tell what is in them. But it is not so with broken hearts; when broken hearts sing, they do sing. When broken hearts groan, they do groan. Broken hearts never play at repenting, nor play at believing.[7]

Penitential tears, while important, do not bring about redemption, but rather are the fruit of it. If you are a born-again believer, you have been redeemed; you have been bought by the blood of Christ. You have repented from your sin, and you have turned to run on the straight and narrow toward the Savior of your soul. Your repentance was a onetime event that signified your understanding as to why you needed a savior, and it was in that very moment that you were transferred from the kingdom of darkness into the kingdom of light in the Son. So, while there is no need to challenge your security as a child of God through repeatedly repenting, we are called to confess our sin over and over until the day we are made whole in the presence of our Maker. I am confident I was safe and secure in my salvation when I was in the battle of my life with suicidal ideation; however, I still needed to confess ruminating on suicide, for there is no freedom from those evil commands without lamenting my sinfulness to the Lord. And not to earn my salvation, but rather to voice my agreement with God in just how ugly my sin was.

Now, let's look at David's lament in Psalm 6, where his difficult circumstances opened his eyes to the sin in his life, leading him to confession.

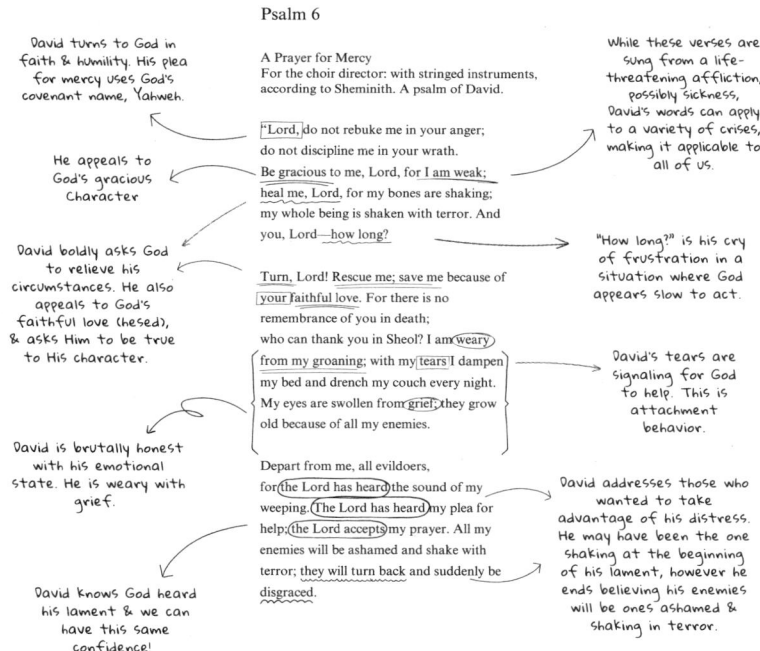

David's honest confession fostered intimacy with the God who collects his tears and does not let one roll down his cheek unnoticed. Paul's letter to the Corinthians is beautifully applicable here. He says: "For godly grief *and* the pain God is permitted to direct, produce a repentance that leads *and* contributes to salvation *and* deliverance from evil, and it never brings regret; but worldly grief (the hopeless sorrow that is characteristic of the pagan world) is deadly [breeding and ending in death]" (2 Cor. 7:10 AMPC). "This godly grief is an emotional experience ignited by concern not at what people see but at what God sees. It is not sorrow at being caught in sin; it is sorrow at being in sin. Godly grief terminates not in hardness of heart but in penitence. Grief 'according to God' pushes one up toward heaven and restored fellowship with God and thus with others, not down into the loneliness of despair of self-justification. Godly grief does not end in grief; it flows beyond the sorrow into repentance and regained joy."[8] When we bring that which has been sinfully cherished in the dark out into the light, fellowship is restored with God. The Enemy wants you to turn in shame like Judas did, but remember, God already sees every single sin, for Psalm 90:8 (AMPC) says, "Our iniquities, our secret heart *and* its sins [which we would so like to conceal even from ourselves], You have set in the [revealing] light of Your countenance." And what's even more amazing is that He loves us anyway.

Did I still struggle with tempting thoughts when I first started to turn to God in lament? Of course. I'm human. But as I turned back to Him over and over again, He purified my heart and led me in the way of lamenting the sin I was savoring.

And in keeping with the Puritan prayer at the start of this chapter, "let the bones that you have broken rejoice" (Ps. 51:8b ESV).

Reflection Questions

1. Are the penitential psalms a new idea for you?

2. In your own words, explain the role of lament in confessing your sin.

3. Is there a sin pattern in your life that you feel stuck in? If so, how might the penitential psalms guide you in confessing your sin to the Lord?

Now it's your turn. Grab a journal and write your own lament. In appendix 1 you'll find words that may help you describe what you're feeling, and in appendix 2, you'll find a guide for response and prayer as you reflect on this chapter.

PART 3

Implications for the Church

CHAPTER 10

Lamenting Together

*Help us, O God of our salvation,
for the glory of your name.*

PSALM 79:9a ESV

The tornado siren eerily filled the silence in our home. The pitch-black darkness concealed the tornado in the distance; however, the whistling wind tearing shingles off my neighbor's home and lifting up our backyard shed made its presence known. I hurried the kids into our shelter as the sound of hail ricocheted off our garage door. My cell phone lost service as we closed ourselves in our small, metal refuge. My husband was in another state, and I was out of my comfort zone without him. Although the siren continued, no cell service meant no idea where that beast of a twister was.

Somehow, my neighbor's text made it through. She and two other neighbors needed shelter, so I unlocked ours, climbed out, and opened the garage door. Violent rain soaked me as belongings stashed around me were instantly wet. I was safe since I would later learn significant damage started about half a mile away; however, I didn't know I was safe. My neighbors ran down the street and into our shelter, and as I waited for the garage door to close, a huge clap of thunder scared me down the stairs faster than I knew possible. The neighbor slammed the shelter door over us, locking it as I sighed in relief. It didn't matter what was happening on the other side of that door; my children and I were hidden away in our shelter and a sense of comfort came over me. When all sounded calm, we made our way out of the shelter, unaware of what we'd find on the other side. Although only acquainted with our neighbors, as we walked around our street inspecting each other's homes, camaraderie comforted my anxiety. We had just been through a tornado together; we were not alone in our experience. Other neighbors joined us, and at a time of night when we'd normally be locked away in the privacy of our own homes, there we were, *together*.

A few days after the tornado, I headed out of town for a Christian women's retreat. Upon leaving our town and entering the next, I realized the rest of the world was operating per usual. The contrast of destruction behind me and normal life around me was disorienting. I craved those back home who understood my sorrow and shock. Trauma concealed by a smile left me feeling incongruent and on the verge of giving into flight. Joining the laughter of women around me didn't heal my broken heart, for we know that "Laughter can conceal a heavy heart, but when the laughter ends, the grief remains" (Prov. 14:13 NLT). However, one by one, I began to cross paths with others from my town in that huge conference center. Each embrace carried comfort. But is just knowing you aren't alone enough?

Soon after the retreat, I was back home in church on Sunday morning. Wearied faces wore stress for all to see. As worship began, the lyrics "my comfort, my shelter . . ." flashed on the screen, causing me to freeze mid-sentence. God as my shelter had never resonated much with me. Until now. Trauma, like a tornado, has a way of changing your perspective. While anxious, wet, afraid, and alone without my husband during the tornado, I really was safe because I was in my shelter—with my true Shelter. My contemplations in church strengthened my secure attachment to God. Storm shelters save lives, but if your storm shelter is full of snakes and leaks, it would be scarier to run to in the midst of a deadly tornado. Honestly, one might have to weigh their options and decided what's worse—a shelter full of things that could hurt you, or the tornado itself. Just like emotionally healthy parents, running to a clean and secure shelter is a haven from havoc. And just as a group runs for safety in a storm shelter, our group of believers at church were running to God, our refuge, in our time of need. That morning, people chatted, exchanged stories from the tornado, prayed with one another, and cried, yet came back together as a church and worshipped our sovereign Lord *together*. We were lamenting the loss and destruction in our community *as a community*. Hebrews 10:25 (NLT) encourages us to "not neglect our meeting together, as some people do, but encourage one another, especially now that the day of his return is drawing near." We are in this Christian life together, and it most certainly is a community endeavor. We seek God together, we study His Word together, we worship together, we pray together, we grieve together, we lament together, and we persevere together.

I finally saw that knowing you're not alone in a community tragedy is good, but lamenting that tragedy as a community is better. The Enemy wants isolated saints suffocating in their pain, unaware that lament is even an option. We weren't doing that. Hearing others voice anguish, and even confusion, as to why a tornado will destroy one house, yet not touch the neighbor's house, helped me feel seen in my own questions. God saw each and every tear that morning. In David's lament to God, recorded in Psalm 56, he affirms this: "You yourself have recorded my wanderings. Put my tears in your bottle. Are they not in your book?" (v. 8). And God wants you to let others see your tears as well.

Tears

There are three types of tears: basal, reflex, and emotional. With each blink, basal tears are spread over the surface of your eye, keeping them from drying out. They work to flush debris out of the eye, such as dust, dirt, and germs, and help ensure clear vision. Reflex tears act as a rapid way to flush out irritants such as smoke or onion. Emotional tears "arise from strong emotions. Empathy, compassion, physical pain, attachment pain, and moral and sentimental emotions can trigger these tears. They communicate your emotions to others. Emotional tears make you feel more vulnerable, which could improve your relationships. Crying often connects people, whether it's out of passion, or another strong emotion. Crying may cause others to be empathetic and compassionate toward you, softening anger or unpleasant emotion that caused the tears to flow in the first place."[1] Tears are a critical aspect of human connection, not only signaling to others that you are vulnerable, but inviting them to be vulnerable as well. "Crying has also been shown to increase attachment behavior, encouraging closeness, empathy, and support from friends and family."[2]

If your thoughts and emotions were invalidated as a child, you're likely to feel guilt for having them. Expressing emotion, including crying, is both healthy and cathartic; however, for many cultures around the world, showing emotion is considered taboo. In an attempt to provide a space for people to embrace vulnerability and experience the healing power of tears, Japanese entrepreneur, Hiroki Terai, began offering a crying service that provided a way for people to experience the benefits of crying *together*. "The sessions are called rui-katsu, or 'tear-seeking,' a therapeutic practice for women that is said to relieve stress levels and bring people together. After much research into the benefits of crying, Terai developed his own methodology to induce tears from his clients and finally launched his therapy business in 2015."[3]

And speaking of therapy, did you know that while there is individual therapy available, there is another approach called group therapy? Many groups are created to target a specific problem or struggles such as substance abuse, depression, anxiety, or even those who have experienced something like losing a loved one to suicide. It can be intimidating to consider joining a group; however, there are certain advantages unique to group therapy that individual therapy may not offer, including gleaning coping ideas from others, as well as accountability. The group is led by a trained professional, but there is something uniquely comforting about being with others and knowing you aren't the only one who struggles. Talking and listening to others also has a way of putting your own struggles and problems in perspective. "Diversity is another important benefit of group therapy. People have different personalities and backgrounds, and they look at situations in different ways. By seeing how other people tackle problems and make positive changes, you can discover a whole range of strategies for facing your own concerns."[4]

The benefits are undeniable, and the science behind group therapy is validated by Scripture. But could there be a way to deepen the impact of group therapy for believers by adding lament to the experience? Widows coming together to witness each other's pain, lament to God together, and then spur one another on in trusting God as their Provider would offer comfort like nothing else. Some of the women may have lost husbands after fifty years of marriage, and some after only one. Some may have lost their husbands due to old age, and some at war. The women may come from different financial situations, cultures, and generations; however, loss has a way of uniting hearts in a way that breaks barriers. And lamenting loss goes even further in connecting hearts with one another and to the Father. The importance of diversity in group therapy, or a support group at church, reflects the intentional diversity God has created within the church as a whole. We are one body, made up of many parts, whose importance is equal. "Yes, the body has many different parts, not just one part. If the foot says, 'I am not a part of the body because I am not a hand,' that does not make it any less a part of the body. And if the ear says, 'I am not part of the body because I am not an eye,' would that make it any less a part of the body? If the whole body were an eye, how would you hear? Or if your whole body were an ear, how would you smell anything?" (1 Cor. 12:14–17 NLT). Your specific gifting is needed to encourage and build up the church, but so is your ability to love and support others in the way only you can. You are not meant to endure adversity in isolation, but rather as a group, or family, whose collective cry is welcomed by God. "So if one member suffers, all the members suffer with it; if one member is honored, all the members rejoice with it" (v. 26). "When one body part suffers, the whole body suffers. Whether an arm is broken or a tooth aches or an ankle is sprained or the lower back is sore or our head aches, that injury affects the entire body—not just one isolated body part.[5]

If revealing our pain to others is good, and lamenting it with others is better, where do we begin in knowing what to pray if this is an uncomfortable concept? We go to Scripture, where God has provided us with multiple examples to follow.

Psalm 90 is a community lament based on some disaster where God's people call on Him for help.

> Return, O LORD! How long?
>   Have pity on your servants!
> Satisfy us in the morning with your steadfast love,
>   that we may rejoice and be glad all our days.

> Make us glad for as many days as you have afflicted
> us,
> and for as many years as we have seen evil.
> Let your work be shown to your servants,
> and your glorious power to their children.
> Let the favor of the Lord our God be upon us,
> and establish the work of our hands upon us;
> yes, establish the work of our hands!
> (vv. 13–17 ESV)

Psalm 44 is a community lament for when God's people as a whole have endured some great tragedy inflicted upon them by enemies. The first thing that comes to my mind as a way to apply this lament are the attacks on 9/11:

> Wake up, Lord! Why are you sleeping?
> Get up! Don't reject us forever!
> Why do you hide
> and forget our affliction and oppression?
> For we have sunk down to the dust;
> our bodies cling to the ground.
> Rise up! Help us!
> Redeem us because of your faithful love.
> (vv. 23–26)

Psalm 83 is a community lament appropriate for a situation when believers are being threatened by others. This psalm asks God to intervene and foil the plans of their enemies. "Christians would use this psalm not against 'national enemies' (Christians transcend national boundaries) but in cases where their persecutors would destroy them and all traces of their faith."[6] When used rightly, this lament seeking help from God would be sung by believers as a witness so that their persecutors might come to know the Lord.

> Make them like tumbleweed, my God,
> like straw before the wind.
> As fire burns a forest,
> as a flame blazes through mountains,
> so pursue them with your tempest
> and terrify them with your storm.
> Cover their faces with shame
> so that they will seek your name, Lord.
> Let them be put to shame and terrified forever;
> let them perish in disgrace.
> May they know that you alone—
> whose name is the Lord—
> are the Most High over the whole earth.
> (vv. 13–18)

Lamenting pain that is experienced by a community, as a community, is important, just as lamenting personal pain individually to God is. But there is one more scenario I believe is important, and that is lamenting individual pain within community. I discovered this in the basement of my church on a Tuesday morning when one woman's brave lament left me changed forever.

Empathetic Witness

In the Spring of 2022, I felt led to teach a short series on lament to the women's Bible study at my church. One morning I provided note cards on each table for women to write down their own lament. I eventually asked if anyone would be willing to read their lament to the class. One brave woman accepted my challenge. She began by addressing God in faith, but quickly moved to expressing her deep pain over miscarriages and struggles with infertility. Through tears, she invited us to witness her pain and confusion as she lamented to the Lord. Crying is attachment behavior, and surely at the sight of her tears, our attachment as a safe sisterhood was strengthened. It was as though she had cracked the door to her prayer closet and let us peek in as she laid her soul bare before her Father. She and her husband love God, pursue holiness, and share the gospel with others consistently. They would provide a loving home for children, and yet her arms remain empty. Why, Lord? How long, Lord? I looked around the room and noticed other women crying. Were they struggling with infertility too? Were they longing for their babies born into heaven decades prior? As her lament transitioned from voicing her pain to declaring her trust, my faith was strengthened. She sat down and I stood astounded at what I had just witnessed. Honestly, prior to her lament, I saw her smiling and serving at church. Due to her joyful disposition, I didn't realize the grief she carried in place of a baby. But now when I see her joy, I see the miracle of it. Now when I see her serve in the nursery, I see God as her Sustainer. Now when I see her looking sad, I know to stop and ask her about it. Her Tuesday lament went further than just connecting her heart to God; it connected it to others—others who now knew how to pray for her, encourage her, and hold her accountable. And what's even more beautiful is that now, as I'm writing this, she and her husband are in the process of adopting a group of sisters. Seeing her nurture them in the hallway at church, knowing the grief that surely remains in her heart, grows my faith. On that Tuesday morning, she wasn't the only woman to lament in front of the group. Her vulnerability sparked courage in others, and one by one, women took their turn lamenting raw emotion, stripped of any fanfare, to God in front of a sisterhood of empathetic witnesses.

Excruciating pain can swallow up all order and connection you once felt; however, when someone bears witness to your pain, they are essentially communicating that you are not alone in it. This is one of the reasons emotional and verbal abuse is so harmful—it often goes unseen and, therefore, victims can live their entire lives in turmoil, possibly not even understanding they were abused as a child. When something tragic happens to you, it can break your sense of belonging. When I was with my friends after my mom died, I felt like I didn't belong because they all had their moms. When my dad died by suicide, I felt like I didn't belong, because even if friends had lost their dads, suicide is just different than natural causes of death. Looking back now, I understand why I felt so alone. However, grief is universal, and while it comes in various shades, we all understand what it feels like to hurt. You can be an empathetic witness to another's pain even if you haven't directly experienced their loss. "Belonging and being loved are core to the human experience. We are a social species; we are meant to be in community—emotionally, socially, and physically interconnected with the others."[7]

In a culture of burying feelings, expressing them and having them witnessed by another can be awkward. Knowing how to respond to someone grieving can be even scarier. If you want to help your grieving loved one, learn to lament. Lament is the comforting way to pull them close and give them vocabulary to go to God when words most likely fail them. Loss can be confusing, terrifying, and a thief of words. Rather than trite phrases like "just have faith," that are a flimsy bandage at best, salt on their wounds at worst, lament offers a real way to express pain and run to the throne of mercy, *together*, in their time of need. Perhaps your loved one will lament with you, but you may be the one lamenting on their behalf. This will undoubtedly draw their gaze to Christ, the ultimate empathetic witness, and help them know how to begin to verbalize their deep distress to Him. God has extended the invitation to His children to draw near to Him, but sometimes that is learned through drawing near to another believer who bears His image.

Knowing that Jesus understands our pain paves the way for us to embrace confidence to turn to God, "For we do not have a high priest who is unable to sympathize with our weaknesses, but one who has been tempted in every way as we are, yet without sin" (Heb. 4:15). Jesus understands the entire scope of human emotion. He understands what it's like to be loved, rejected, abused, comforted, tempted, hated, brought in, and cast out. Because of this, we really can lay aside fear of rejection, or the fear that He simply won't understand, as we draw near to Him.

Groaning Together

The beginning of Exodus was characterized by oppression, slavery, and death, with deliverance and freedom being major themes after Exodus 2. The shift happened, though, when God heard the groans of His people.

> The Israelites groaned because of their difficult labor, they cried out, and their cry for help because of the difficult labor ascended to God. God heard their groaning, and God remembered his covenant with Abraham, with Isaac, and with Jacob. God saw the Israelites, and God knew. (Exod. 2:23b–25)

God heard. God remembered. God saw them. God knew. God is the ultimate empathic witness, but more than that, He is the ultimate empathetic deliverer.

Groaning is the universal response to grief, grave oppression, and despair. Groaning is the guttural sound from those whose pain is so overwhelming that words escape them. And in Exodus, the groans were communal. Groans can also be individual, but just as God's people groaned together in Egypt, we still groan together today:

> For we know that the whole creation has been groaning together in the pains of childbirth until now. And not only the creation, but we ourselves, who have the firstfruits of the Spirit, groan inwardly as we wait eagerly for adoption as sons, the redemption of our bodies. For in this hope we were saved. Now hope that is seen is not hope. For who hopes for what he sees? But if we hope for what we do not see, we wait for it with patience.
>
> Likewise the Spirit helps us in our weakness. For we do not know what to pray for as we ought, but the Spirit himself intercedes for us with groanings too deep for words. (Rom. 8:22–26 ESV)

Here, Paul describes the groaning condition of God's entire creation, and not just a small portion of it. Groaning together is a collective lamentation. Yes, as believers we praise God together, but we also languish together, and will do so until our faith is made sight. All of creation, including us, groans together as a woman in labor. But labor doesn't last forever. And neither will our pain.

We groan because of the way sin ravages lives, and because tragedy happens. We groan because people remain addicted and stuck in unhealthy cycles. We groan because people reject God and die, and we groan because loved ones take their lives, and children are kidnapped. All of it makes us groan, and really, our groans are the hopeful way believers live in the tension of the already and not yet. Jesus felt this same tension and groaned too. "We might overlook this remarkable moment in the human life of Christ—his groaning aloud in Mark 7:34—if it didn't happen again, and with more intensity, just a few verses later in Mark 8:12. That is, twice, just paragraphs apart—first before the feeding of the four thousand, then again immediately after—'Jesus sighed.' And the second instance was more dramatic than the first ('he sighed deeply in his spirit'). The Greek for *sigh* (*stenazō*) we translate *groan* elsewhere in the New Testament."[8] We see in story after story that Jesus experienced human emotion. He not only groaned like us, but His sighing was for us. I groan because I have lost my dad to suicide, but when a friend tells me she just lost her dad to suicide, I groan for her. Because I know what it feels like. Groaning, or sighing, is the sound of grief. Lament is putting the grief into words, and while Jesus did lament, there were times that He simply sighed. And we can too. But remember, God hears your groans, Jesus understands your groans, and the Spirit groans with and for you. "For we do not know what to pray for as we ought, but the Spirit himself intercedes for us with groanings too deep for words (Rom. 8:26 ESV).

David said, "I am weary from my groaning; with my tears I dampen my bed and drench my couch every night" (Ps. 6:6). If this is you too, you are in good company within the pages of Scripture. Remember you aren't alone. You have us. You have God, and you have the Spirit who groans with and for you.

Reflection Questions

1. Why do you think lamenting within community is important?

2. Have you ever been through a tragedy as a community that was lamented by the community?

3. Do you see any form of community lament happening within your church?

Now it's your turn. Grab a journal and write your own lament. In appendix 1 you'll find words that may help you describe what you're feeling, and in appendix 2, you'll find a guide for response and prayer as you reflect on this chapter.

CHAPTER 11

Missional Lament

"I am the LORD, *and there is no other.*
form light and create darkness; I make well-being and
create calamity; I am the LORD, *who does all these things."*

ISAIAH 45:6b–7 ESV

The majority of this book is focused on lamenting pain to God, both individually and communally, but the hope is that it doesn't stop there. If we are intimately attached to God, and each other, which is one of the outcomes of lament, the effect will be worldwide in scope. Life is hard, mental health struggles can linger for years, and yet we are not excused from playing our part in hastening Christ's return. To maintain focus on fulfilling the Great Commission, we must prioritize the pursuit of mental and emotional health, for childhood trauma can certainly complicate loving others. I first learned this as a new missionary, when I witnessed a Turkish woman being slapped and yelled at in public and immediately flashed back to when my dad would yell at me. This was paralyzing, and precisely why we lament and ask the hard questions that plague us all if we are going to remain engaged in sharing Christ. There is a place for you in ministry, and I believe your most effective work will likely flow from your deepest wounds, but in order to truly thrive, we must lament. And this is how I came to believe that.

Earthquake

"No, no, no," is all I could utter under my breath as I watched a video of the earthquake that hit southern Turkey, the country we called home as missionaries, on February 6, 2023. I felt the paradox of the Internet as I sat glued to my phone. Seeing the unfolding disaster was a blessing in that I knew how to pray for my Turkish friends. However, being in Oklahoma, unable to help, felt like a curse. Safely sitting in the comfort of my American home felt like reverse culture shock. Like an itchy woolen sweater on sensitive skin, I felt chafed by my physical reality. Or maybe sackcloth is a more accurate analogy. I yearned to be in Turkey as a herald of hope in despair, helping hands in destruction, and grounding hugs in trauma, but now I lived in the US. That unique heart split occurs when you live somewhere, and roots grow deep regardless of your citizenship. The inner tug-of-war was a thread of discord in my soul, only to be further tangled when well-meaning churchgoers would later say, "I'm so glad you're here where it's safe, and not there." I'd politely smile and nod for the most part, while secretly questioning if they understood the cost of following Jesus:

> Jesus said to His disciples, If anyone desires to be My disciple, let him deny himself [disregard, lose sight of, and forget himself and his own interests] and take up his cross and follow Me [cleave steadfastly to Me, conform wholly to My example in living and, if need be, in dying, also].
>
> For whoever is bent on saving his [temporal] life [his comfort and security here] shall lose it [eternal life]; and whoever loses his life [his comfort and security here] for My sake shall find it [life everlasting]. (Matt. 16:24–25 AMPC)

Authentic discipleship is costly, but lamenting through the grief on your way to glory is essential; it's how we steward our feelings well as we take up our cross and follow Him. I wanted to be there, and really, I wanted God to do something. To act. To intervene. My heart's lament sounded much like David's: "Arise, O Lord!" (Ps. 3:7 ESV).

I frantically scrolled through videos, irrationally hoping they weren't real. The recipe reels I typically wasted my time watching remained replaced by terrifying videos in real time. I once stood where bodies were now buried. As homes became graves, survivors were traumatized in a terrain whose former heavenly beauty now resembled a hellish war zone. I boosted the volume on the videos. I not only understood the heart behind the horrified screams that transcended language barriers, but having learned Turkish, I understood their very words. This ushered in unique, isolating grief as my friends in Oklahoma couldn't relate. I listened to moms scream for missing children kidnapped by the earthquake while staring at their home in a heap. Can you imagine having nervous breakdowns broadcast for the entire world to see? There's a famous image of a father sitting next to rubble, holding his trapped, dead daughter's hand. This photograph proves what they say to be true, a photograph is worth a thousand words. And then there were the murmurs through the grapevine of a Christian Turkish couple that died, leaving behind a young son to be raised in a Muslim culture. With so few Muslim-background believers in the area, why would God take them from the work permanently? It makes no sense.

Grief. So much confusing and complicated grief.

How long, Lord, will these buildings keep falling? Why would You take babies from mothers and leave children orphaned with no one to help them? I can't stand it. Please, God, do something. I trust You, for

> *no disaster surprises You. You are a father to the fatherless. You are in complete control with ways that are higher than ours.*

Lamenting alone in my room was good, but it wasn't until I reached out to a few former missionaries in a group message that my sorrow remembered its hope. They weren't disconnected from the destruction in Turkey like those who had never been there. They also once stood on that now devastated ground and they, too, had friends directly affected and possibly no longer alive. Some of them survived prior earthquakes in Turkey while serving the Lord, adding a layer of complication to their sorrow that was not lost on me. Their steadfast trust in God fueled my own, and their hope inspired me to hold fast to mine. Grief was still there, but my strength in the midst of it grew. I watched the story unfold for a long time after our messages tapered off, but something in me shifted as we bore witness to each other's pain, which surely fanned the flame of our collective faith.

Watching live streams of the aftershocks wasn't even the worst part. It was being confronted with the agonizing reality that statistically very few of the more than 55,000 casualties knew Christ as their Savior. Had they even had the chance to hear the gospel? But regardless, according to God's words through Paul's pen, they were without excuse: "For his invisible attributes, that is, his eternal power and divine nature, have been clearly seen since the creation of the world, being understood through what he has made. As a result, people are without excuse" (Rom. 1:20).

> *Oh Lord, how is this fair? How can You explicitly let me hear the gospel when others don't get that same opportunity? Why do I get Scripture in my language and others don't? Why would You take us from the mission field when we could be sharing with them?*

Please send people to share the gospel with the survivors. Open their eyes. I don't understand, but I am choosing to trust we are supposed to be in Oklahoma right now.

Lamenting latched my heart to God as I wrestled within my human limitation. I resonated with Jeremiah's lament over his people's deceitful ways when he said, "My joy is gone; grief is upon me; my heart is sick within me" (Jer. 8:18 ESV). We are given a template here of how to grieve what grieves God, and it grieves God when those bearing His image rebel against Him, and reject Him altogether. How do we grieve without hope for them, though? Yes, we do not grieve as others do, for as believers, no matter what happens on earth, we personally have a living hope the world does not have. Grief for those who didn't share our hope is painful, and unfortunately easier to push aside and avoid. Were there Muslims in that earthquake who had heard the gospel and didn't believe? Did God know they didn't need another chance to repent? Surely He did, for He is infinitely wise and searches the heart of men. Ezekiel 18, which speaks to personal responsibility when it comes to sin, teaches that God doesn't delight when unbelievers die (v. 23), but even so, my heart was sick within me. Avoiding these questions and emotions becomes like a pressure cooker. Turning to God, asking the questions, and feeling what you feel opens the valve, allowing for dysregulated emotion to find release in the realm of faith. It may not take away your feelings; however, it will provide stability within them. As we lament, we must lament on the foundation that "Even if he causes suffering, he will show compassion according to the abundance of his faithful love. For he does not enjoy bringing affliction or suffering on mankind" (Lam. 3:32–33).

And then there were the believers who died in the earthquake. We also grieve differently than the world in that when a believer dies, we know that they are alive in the presence of Christ, fully healed in perfect joy. We must remember, though, that ignoring emotion, because we know the glorious end of the story, is unhealthy. God made emotion to be felt and expressed rather than numbed and repressed. Dismissing pain over the death of saints is not godliness, and joy in the wake of death, without its companion, sorrow, is unrealistic. Grieving with hope still hurts. God created grief as a way for you to process loss, and Jesus didn't hide His. I would argue that being honest with the scope of your emotions to God is not only the godly way to steward the feelings He designed humans to experience, but it shows the world that God is a safe place to be yourself. It's good and right to mourn over the death of saints even while fully assured they are in a better place, for even after Stephen victoriously kept his eyes locked on heaven while being martyred, "Devout men buried Stephen and made great lamentation over him" (Acts 8:2 ESV).

Deuteronomy 29:29 (ESV) says, "The secret things belong to the LORD our God, but the things that are revealed belong to us and our children forever, that we may do all the words of this law." God doesn't have to tell us everything, which doesn't negate His goodness, but rather proves that He is, in fact, higher than His creation. In the same way we don't know everything God knows, it's not healthy or necessary for children to know everything a parent knows. Our children obey us based on the foundation of trust that has been built through our proven faithfulness. And so it is with God. "Not everything that is true of God has been revealed. That there are secret things anticipates the need to trust, obey, and be humble before God. What God has revealed is for the sake of obedience."[1] The mysterious aspects of God are not intended to produce emotionless, mindless robots in us, for even a heart walking by faith would be remiss not to acknowledge what it feels. When my securely attached kids feel frustrated, and ask me "why," it fosters relationship and speaks of the safety they feel with me. Sometimes I explain the reason, but other times the best answer I can give them is, "Just trust me." God may act unpredictably, but even so, we can wail in sorrow and still obey our trustworthy God from a settled security found in our faith.

Paul described himself in 2 Corinthians 4:8b by saying, "we are perplexed but not in despair." The Greek word for *perplexed* means to be "without resource. Figuratively, to doubt, hesitate, be perplexed, not knowing how to proceed, determine, speak, or act."[2] The secret things that belong to God may leave us perplexed, but when we turn and tell Him in trust, we find a safeguard against despair. We join the father whose son was possessed by a demon in Mark 9:24 in saying, "I do believe; help my unbelief!" Lament is the language of the good fight of faith, and it's a necessary aspect of staying in the mission of winning souls for Christ when God's ways don't make sense.

In a friendly conversation with a scribe, Jesus answered his question regarding which commandment is the most important by saying, "The most important is Listen, Israel! The Lord our God, the Lord is one. Love the Lord your God with all your heart, with all your soul, with all your mind, and with all your strength. The second is, Love your neighbor as yourself. There is no other command greater than these" (Mark 12:29–31). To love your neighbor as yourself is to desire their salvation. Contemplating the eternal destination of those who die as enemies of Yahweh creates a concoction of fear and frustration, with anger and sadness in the mix. Jesus said, "I am the way, the truth, and the life. No one comes to the Father except through me" (John 14:6). Having lived in Turkey, a predominately Muslim country, I struggle with this reality. When the lost who die are those you love, allegiance to God's sovereignty can wane. Do I accept God's declaration that only the born-again will enter His presence after death, or do I allow my attachment to unbelieving family and friends cause me to reject this truth? The Word speaks of the Savior by saying, "This Jesus is the stone rejected by you builders, which has become the cornerstone. There is salvation in no one else, for there is no other name under heaven given to people by which we must be saved" (Acts 4:11–12). Because Jesus is the only way, dying without faith in Him means entrance into heaven is not their reality. This is already hard to grapple with, only complicated by a loving God who allows something like an earthquake to kill thousands of unbelievers without warning.

> *Why did You allow such a disaster in Turkey, Lord? I'm angry that some heard the gospel and rejected it. Can't You give them more time? Why are children still being raised to reject Christ? Do something! But I trust in Your perfect plan, "For I know that the Lord is great; our Lord is greater than all gods. The Lord does whatever he pleases in heaven and on earth, in the seas and all the depths" (Ps. 135:5–6), and everything You do is wise and loving.*

First Timothy 2:4 says God "wants everyone to be saved and to come to the knowledge of the truth." Is it even possible to stay engaged in the Great Commission when we experience sudden loss of those we've given our lives to reach? Yes, there are times when God's desires appear incongruent with the destruction He allows, but we must keep our eyes locked on Jesus, the pioneer and perfecter of faith (Heb. 12:2). We can tell Him, appeal to Him, and choose to trust Him. It may not make sense, but this is what it looks like to walk by faith and not by sight (2 Cor. 5:7). As we leave room for Jesus to author and nurture the faith of others, we in turn see Him do the same for our faith. "I am sure of this, that he who started a good work in you will carry it on to completion until the day of Christ Jesus" (Phil. 1:6), and so the journey may be long as you learn to articulate your sorrow to the Man of Sorrows, but I'm confident that as you do, you'll learn that sorrow taken to God becomes sweetened with joy and infused with hope.

Staying on Mission

I held my kids close while waiting for a taxi near a shopping mall in Istanbul. We had been living there long enough to understand our way around, but were still new enough to be surprised at what was about to take place. Without warning, screams from a teenaged girl captured our attention, and I instinctively covered my daughter's eyes. An angry man, presumably her dad, was dragging her by her ponytail, yelling at her, and hitting her in the head. As a foreigner, I remember frantically looking to bystanders and being struck by their lack of action. Why was no one helping her? PTSD reared its ugly head, and while my dad never hit me with his hand, he did with his words. The girl broke free and beelined to a security guard, but my sigh of relief morphed into horror as the guard pushed her back to her dad. That was the moment I realized I was not promised help should the need arise. The little girl in me who felt that she had no one to help her in childhood showed up within me. Personal trauma can surely complicate ministry, but this is why we must lament. Our longevity depends on it.

Watching no one help that girl was distressing. I had no way of knowing that several years later, I would be the girl who needed help to escape two men while others merely watched them take advantage of me. After being shattered by those men who treated me with zero respect on a train at night, I timidly opened up to another believer about what happened to me. Her first response was: "Well what does Jesus say to do? He says to forgive." She was correct; however, her dismissal of my emotion heaped shame on me for feeling angry, violated, scared, and sad. And so, in a moment ripe for learning and practicing lament, I avoided what I felt in the name of forgiveness. Choosing silence was also a way to save face, for I thought, "What missionary struggles to forgive?" Every missionary is human; therefore, all of them do. I didn't understand that I could forgive those men and also tell God how hurtful and scary that experience was. I would later unpack what happened on that train in Istanbul with my therapist; however, the years of avoidance came at a cost. I hope you consider mine a cautionary tale and turn to God, rather than away.

The girl at the mall wasn't our first experience seeing women abused. Upon our initial arrival to Turkey, I remember putting my son to sleep while hearing a woman crying, a man yelling, and things being thrown directly below his bedroom. The violent arguments were impossible to ignore as was the helplessness I felt while I laid on the hardwood floor, ear to the ground, and prayed for that family. But here's the problem: my prayers were incomplete. I asked God to help that family, but I never told Him how distressed I felt, or how angry I was that He was allowing her abuse. I didn't tell Him how triggering that was in view of my childhood. He already knew, but I missed out on the intimacy found when we communicate our feelings to God and experience His lavish comfort in return. I lived in a state of hypervigilance and helplessness rather than hopefulness. Helplessness. This may very well have been one of the most trying emotions I experienced as a missionary. Having your comfort, and even rights, stripped away tends to teach you just how little control you have in changing hearts, stopping pain, shielding your family from trauma, ignoring your own trauma, and even communicating at times.

And speaking of trauma, the Islamic State gained global prominence in 2014, less than a year into our arrival overseas. "The roots of ISIS trace back to 2004, when the organization known as 'al Qaeda in Iraq' formed."[3] Reading of brutal beheadings performed by this group was difficult enough, but it wasn't until the civil war in Syria led to millions of refugees fleeing their home country—oftentimes either to, or by way of, Turkey—that the war became personal. The strategic geographical location of Turkey also made this beautiful country the avenue in which extremists left their homes around the world to enter Syria and join ISIS in their efforts. Hearing of those now trained in terrorist tactics returning to their home countries was terrifying. The whole world went on high alert, including me as a missionary, as I lived in wait for the day that my husband, kids, and I would fall victim to a terrorist attack. When I put my young children on a bus to go to school in Turkey, I often questioned whether or not I would see them again, and if the loss of them was worth it. Jesus said, "If anyone comes to me and does not hate his own father and mother, wife and children, brothers and sisters—yes, and even his own life—he cannot be my disciple. Whoever does not bear his own cross and come after me cannot be my disciple" (Luke 14:26–27). It's hard to understand the requirements of discipleship even when you are a sold-out follower of Christ who has chosen to bear your cross. And so, we cry out to God. Lament is not a forsaking of our allegiance, but rather a gift from God when our hearts and minds war for our affections as authentic disciples.

I continued living my life for the cause of Christ, but hypervigilance intensified within me. It didn't take long for us to befriend refugees who fled Syria in search of safety, and invite them into our home for meals. As true friendships blossomed, they began sharing details of the trauma they had endured. Bombings, terror, sinking boats, discrimination, and family members still trapped there with no reunion on the horizon. These were things I heard about on Netflix, not in real life. My privileged past clapped against my painful present. The friction sanded down my faith. Like a sponge, I soaked up their trauma as if it were mine. I moved to Central Asia assuming I could live immersed in suffering without being touched by it, as if I could walk through water and not get wet.

I learned of secondhand trauma as a missionary, but this phenomenon isn't unique to those ministering on foreign soil. You may be a nurse, pastor, firefighter, foster parent, or even a caregiver for someone struggling with their mental health. Thanks to social media, scrolling videos of disturbing trauma is ever at our fingertips. Live coverage of wars, terrorist attacks, catastrophic weather emergencies, suicides, school shootings, and freak accidents have never been more accessible. I didn't have a label for the weariness I felt as a missionary, but I now understand that secondhand trauma had produced compassion fatigue. Taking in the trauma of others repeatedly was something I attempted to carry alone while exerting great effort in sharing the gospel. Maybe you've heard the expression that it's hard to pour from an empty cup? My cup was empty. My trauma unprocessed. My suicidal thoughts intensifying. My life on the verge of collapse. And my prayers devoid of lament as a way to express it all to my Helper.

In the garden of Gethsemane, Jesus said, "My soul is very sorrowful, even to death" (Matt. 26:38 ESV). Then Jesus lamented to the Father, saying, "If it be possible, let this cup pass from me; nevertheless, not as I will, but as you will" (v. 39 ESV). He then prayed by saying, "My Father, if this cannot pass unless I drink it, your will be done" (v. 42 ESV). In this miraculous portrayal of honesty and humility, Jesus accepts His destiny which entails the horrifying task of bearing the sins of the world, as signified by His use of *this cup*. "The cup in Scripture is symbolic of one's destiny, whether blessing (Ps. 16:5) or disaster (Jer. 25:15), salvation (Ps. 116:13) or wrath (Isa. 51:17)."[4] Jesus models that one who walks in a manner worthy of their calling can do so in both agony and acceptance. When His cup was bitter, He lamented to the Father, which surely helped direct His eyes to the joy set before Him (Heb. 12:2). His pain did not steal His perseverance. Our lamenting King's articulation of sorrow, and brave acceptance of God's plan, is given for our imitation.

There are various ways to battle compassion fatigue, with professional help certainly being one of the most helpful avenues. We were never meant to carry the demands of ministry apart from God's help, but also not without the help of others. In Exodus 18, Moses's father-in-law, Jethro, "rejoiced over all the good things the LORD had done for Israel when he rescued them from the power of the Egyptians. 'Blessed be the LORD,' Jethro exclaimed, 'who rescued you from the power of Egypt and from the power of Pharaoh. He has rescued the people from under the power of Egypt!'" (vv. 9–10). Despite Jethro's celebration, he was curious if Moses's strategy was sustainable. Jethro asked him, "'Why are you alone sitting as judge, while all the people stand around you from morning until evening?' Moses replied to his father-in-law, 'Because the people come to me to inquire of God'" (vv. 14b–15). Jethro's reply is revolutionary: "'What you're doing is not good,' Moses's father-in-law said to him. 'You will certainly wear out both yourself and these people who are with you, because the task is too heavy for you. You can't do it alone'" (vv. 17–18). Much of our task was being done alone given the nature of our ministry, but I was also going at it alone in my own strength, not God's. The culture shock I was confronted by overseas challenged my belief system, and my feelings and questions remained mostly unasked. While my eventual breakdown and hospitalization was years in the making due to the trauma of an unhealthy childhood, my lack of honesty with God certainly hastened our need to move home for healing.

Lament is essential to longevity in ministry, whether it be vocational, in the workplace, or at home with your family. Ministry is tiresome and can be messy. What begins as a dream come true, can end feeling like a nightmare. Being called by God to follow Him to the nations can appear glamorous, but like any job in ministry, the honeymoon phase eventually wears off and life gets real. To walk with others through life, sharing Christ with them and supporting them in a multitude of ways, is a gift of infinite joy and worth; however, it will never be easy. The church you set out to plant may never grow past a few in your lifetime, and you may spend years sharing the gospel in a jungle without ever seeing one salvation. You may be hated for following Christ or experience betrayal from other believers because they are human. You may be traumatized or abused due to where God has sent you, and you may even doubt that God can use you because of your mental health struggles.

So what can we do in the effort to play the long game? We lament; even as those who are entrusted with the gospel, and work tirelessly to share it. We cry. We protest. We accept our humanity and the limitations sovereignly determined by our gracious God. We voice the full scope of our feelings, regardless of how "acceptable" they seem. We call on God for help, and then, we choose the same resolve as our Redeemer when He said, "Nevertheless, not my will, but yours, be done" (Luke 22:42 ESV).

Much like the various psalms of lament, our prayers of sorrow do offer a release, but don't forget they are also rich with theology and doxology. Lament is how we preach truth to ourselves, as we preach truth to others, when everything in us is fighting to believe it. Lamenting to God is how we exercise our faith and see transformative hope cradle our sorrow on the sojourn home to heaven. Human intellect may decide a loving God would never allow atrocity, but remember, our faith does not rest in the wisdom of men, but is a response to the power of God. He is perfectly faithful, and part of His faithfulness has been expressed through including lament in Scripture— namely, throughout the Psalms. They are not shallow pep talks, but rather a glimpse of how other people of God grappled with the reality of who God is, and settled into the rhythm of hopeful, yet maybe even sorrowful, trust. Here is one such song in the night:

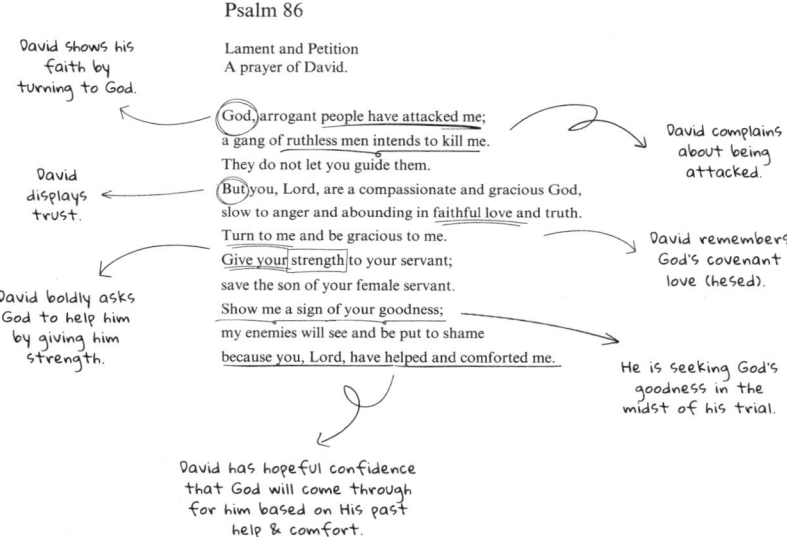

Lament makes life bearable as we wait to see God transform all the smoldering ashes, in our lives and the lives of others, into something beautiful. It's how we stay the course.

Reflection Questions

1. Have you felt disqualified from ministering to others because of your past trauma or your current mental health struggles?

2. Have you ever considered the role of lament in staying engaged in the Great Commission?

3. What is your experience with compassion fatigue?

Now it's your turn. Grab a journal and write your own lament. In appendix 1 you'll find words that may help you describe what you're feeling, and in appendix 2, you'll find a guide for response and prayer as you reflect on this chapter.

EPILOGUE

Remembering with Grace

This book was written with careful, and prayerful, consideration. On one hand, I love my family, and want to honor my dad regardless of his style of parenting and devastating choice to end his life. On the other hand, the stories I've shared are my history, and I believe you can't heal from a story coated in sugar, for that story isn't reality. We all make mistakes, and it pains me to imagine my failings as a mother recorded on the written page. At the same time, I want my kids to share the real version of their testimonies, which will most likely involve their parents in some way. I've prayed for wisdom on how to write the truth in a way that was gracious regarding my father, for in many ways he did provide for me. I have compassion for the trauma he endured, and I recognize that he lived in a time when getting help wasn't what it is today.

At the same time, I wish my childhood had been different, and I live with daily sorrow that accompanies having a parent die by suicide. The Lord has been so kind to open my eyes to destructive patterns passed down to me, and it's only through His provision that I am able to do things differently with my children. I want that same healing for you, and so, I have shared difficult aspects of my story. Sometimes I still feel bound by my dad who asked we not share how he died; however, now that he has stood before God, I imagine he would be my biggest cheerleader in sharing that there is, indeed, hope. While writing, I prayed for God to illuminate which stories I could write from my healing, and which I'd just be venting from my wounding. Stories from healing are helpful to others, whereas venting from your wounds in a public forum is not healthy, or holy, for that matter. I believe this book is what God intended, and every story I chose to share was because the benefit of your healing outweighed the awkwardness of revealing intimate details from a man's life who is no longer here to consent.

Most of the laments covered in this book have been from David, the king of Israel from whom the Messiah would eventually come. But do you remember the circumstances around the moment David became king? God's plan involved the death of Saul, the first king of Israel, as the way David would finally be crowned. Saul and David had a difficult relationship, only further complicated by David's devoted friendship with Saul's son, Jonathan. Saul spent years in conflict with David, even trying to kill him on numerous occasions. Saul's reign came to an end when he died by suicide during a battle with the Philistines that claimed the lives of Saul's sons, including Jonathan.

Upon hearing the news that Saul and Jonathan had died, David, and the men with him, tore their clothes out of grief. The messenger of the news was executed, but the very next thing David did was lament over their deaths, saying it should be taught to the people of Judah (see 2 Sam. 1:17–27). David's beautiful and heroic lament is the thoughtful way he put his grief into words, and it was through lamenting as a community that the people learned how to express their mourning. "As part of the historical records of David's reign, the lament provides lasting evidence of David's innocent ascent to the throne. Though grievously wronged by Saul, David nonetheless chose to remember Saul in a generous way, setting an example of graciously emphasizing the good that someone has done after the person dies."[1] At the same time, though, the truth of Saul's actions regarding David are still recorded in the Bible. Forever.

I've come to believe you can acknowledge the truth, yet do so with graciousness rather than bitterness. When a root of bitterness springs up, it poisons those you love, including your own children. Learning to remember my dad with grace and generosity has taken time, but it has been the way I have helped my children know who their grandpa was. Yes, they know his shortcomings, but they also know he provided me with a home, food, a car, and that he loved onion rings from the Kansas state fair.

My hope for this book is that you will feel permission to look back and face what happened to you as a child. Allow yourself to own your emotion, and feel your grief. Perhaps at the moment, you only feel anger or hatred for how those meant to protect you hurt you. Tell God. Lament those feelings and know their presence does not alter His faithful love for you. I also hope that you won't do this alone, but rather alongside safe and nurturing loved ones who can lament with, and for, you as you heal.

I pray that as you venture back into those younger years, preferably with the guidance from a professional, you will welcome the younger parts of you who have been exiled for your survival. We all have inner children in need of nurturing, and what's amazing is that as we acknowledge their existence and then go on to love, validate, and nurture them in ways they weren't as children, we become healthier, more integrated adults. And this is where compassion for our parents flows from. We begin to see them as the hurting adults they were who may not have had access to help. We begin to see they did the best they could. We begin to see them in a balanced way that honors how they hurt us, but can also celebrate the parts of them that were good.

Even in your sorrow, there is hope. One day, there will be no more grief, and therefore no more lament. That day is what we look forward to with confidence. In the meantime, though, we turn toward our Father in hopeful sorrow, and for the joy set before us, we run our race with endurance.

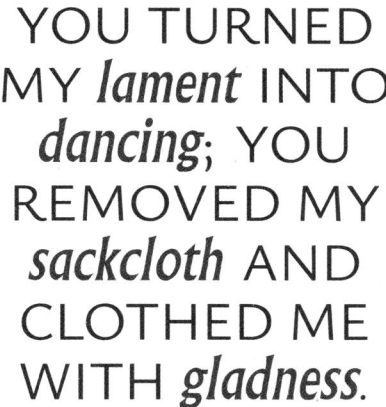

YOU TURNED MY *lament* INTO *dancing*; YOU REMOVED MY *sackcloth* AND CLOTHED ME WITH *gladness*.

PSALM 30:11-12

Acknowledgments

First and foremost, I praise God for teaching me every lesson in this book and giving me the grace to live it out. Being Your daughter is my greatest joy.

Mary Wiley at B&H, thank you for giving me the courage and opportunity to put these lessons into writing. You are an incredible cheerleader and deep source of wisdom. Thank you for believing in me and bringing this message out into the world.

Christine Hoover, I'm thankful for the ways our paths have crossed, and for your willingness to answer my questions along the way. I admire the way you live out your calling, and have learned more from you than you know.

Thank you, Austin Wilson, for your support and guidance during in this process. Working with Wolgemuth & Associates on this project was a dream and answer to prayer.

Christa Carillo Brown, MEd, LPC, this book would not have been possible without you. Thank you for teaching me, remaining patient and compassionate with me, believing me, and celebrating every victory with me. Your prayer life has inspired me in my journey to understand, and practice, lament. My life is better because of you, and every life touched by this message is the fruit of your ministry to me.

I cannot thank board-certified psychiatrist, Dr. Christina Reeder, and board-certified psychiatric nurse practitioner, Alyssa Smith, enough for reviewing my manuscript and supporting this message the Lord has given me. Having experts in the field of psychiatry endorse my work is humbling and encouraging.

Heather Annis, MS, LPC, I also want to thank you for reviewing my manuscript and offering your support and encouragement. I greatly admire you as both a Licensed Professional Counselor, and a follower of Christ. You have played a precious part in my journey.

Last, but certainly not least, I'd love to thank my family. Thank you, Ryan, for your endless support. I am who I am today because you have loved me, cared for me, and have never given up on me. I love our life together. Boston, Evie, Clementine, and Abel, thank you for supporting me during this writing process. You guys have been the best cheerleaders, but more than that, have been the reason I have worked hard to learn and live out the message of this book. May you always feel loved, seen, safe, and known by me as your mother, and may that transfer to you feeling loved, seen, safe, and known by God.

Appendix 1
Words to Help You Lament

Depressed
Anguish
Tired
Empty
Weary
Discouraged
Dejected
Heavy-hearted
Despondent
Sleepy
Depleted
Apathetic
Isolated

Grief
Sorrowful
Angry
Powerless
Miserable
Worried
Shocked
Heartbroken
Hurt
Crushed
Devastated
Numb
Bereaved

Abandoned
Disliked
Unlovable
Deserted
Ignored
Unwelcome
Neglected
Insecure
Insignificant
Inadequate
Worthless
Desperate
Clingy

Abused
Angry
Disgusted
Ashamed
Enraged
Embarrassed
Molested
Helpless
Withdrawn
Trapped
Battered
Exploited
Injured

Upset at God's Ways
Bitter
Confused
Dismayed
Overwhelmed
Anxious
Perplexed
Skeptical
Irritated
Sad
Mad
Resentful
Mystified

Trapped
Scared
Alone
Hopeless
Stuck
Ambushed
Helpless
Imprisoned
Enslaved
Confirmed Stuck
Kidnapped

Purposeless
Aimless

Inadequate
Disappointed
Confused
Adrift
Meaningless
Useless
Empty
Unnecessary
Trivial
Unsuccessful
Unproductive

Anxious

Restless
Tense
Panicky
Uneasy
Frantic
Apprehensive
Nervous
Stressed
Paralyzed
Jittery
Cranky
Edgy

Alone

Lonely
Hurt
Disappointed
Insignificant
Abandoned
Rejected
Excluded
Alienated
Discarded
Sad
Homesick
Envious

Unsafe

Defenseless
Vulnerable
Exposed
Apprehensive
Incapable
Terrified
Doomed
Overpowered
Guarded
Cautious
Wary
Paranoid

Avoidant

Alone
Standoffish
Reserved
Distant
Cold
Aloof
Apprehensive
Insecure
Antisocial
Withdrawn
Independent
Guarded

Suicidal

Hopeless
Scared
Ashamed
Despair
Unwanted
Unneeded
Isolated
Detached
Worthless
Remorseful
Burdensome
Desperate

Dysregulated

Chaotic
Stressed Out
Hopeless
Uncontrolled
Anxious
Unbalanced
Frantic
Panicked
Impulsive
Tangled
Irritable
Confused

Rejected

Abandoned
Unwanted
Isolated
Unseen
Unvalued
Dejected
Deserted
Spurned
Tainted
Neglected
Discarded
Hated

Breaking the Cycle

Grief
Angry
Burdened
Trapped
Doubtful
Betrayed
Unsure
Insecure
Furious
Uncomfortable
Awkward

APPENDIX 2

Reflection Prompts

Use the following prompts as you finish reading each chapter to help guide your time with the Lord, reflecting on what you read and what He is doing through the words in you.

Turn to God

_____
_____
_____
_____
_____
_____
_____
_____
_____

Complaint

_____
_____
_____

_____
_____
_____
_____
_____

Request

  _____
_____
_____
_____
_____
_____
_____
_____

Choose to Trust

  _____
_____
_____
_____
_____
_____
_____
_____

Bibliography

Allender, Dan B. and Tremper Longman II. *The Cry of the Soul: How Our Emotions Reveal Our Deepest Questions About God.* Colorado Springs: Navpress, 2015.

American Psychiatric Association, *Diagnostic and Statistical Manual of Mental Disorders*, 5th ed., text revision. Washington, DC: American Psychiatric Association Publishing, 2022.

American Psychological Association. "Psychotherapy: Understanding Group Therapy." (October 31, 2019), https://www.apa.org/topics/psychotherapy/group-therapy.

American Psychological Association. "Stress in America 2023." (November 2023), https://www.apa.org/news/press/releases/stress/2023/collective-trauma-recovery.

Baker, Warren and Eugene Carpenter, eds. *The Complete Word Study Dictionary: Old Testament.* Chattanooga: AMG Publishers, 2003.

Beck, Judith S. *Cognitive Behavior Therapy: Basics and Beyond.* 3rd ed. New York: The Guilford Press, 2021.

Benisek, Alexandra. "Why We Cry: The Truth About Tearing Up." *WebMD* (November 23, 2024), accessed August 25, 2024, https://www.webmd.com/balance/why-we-cry-tearing-up.

Bennett, Arthur, ed. *The Valley of Vision: A Collection of Puritan Prayers and Devotions*. Edinburgh: The Banner of Truth Trust, 1988.

Bible Project. "The Loyal Love of God." *Bible Project* (November 2, 2020), https://bibleproject.com/podcast/loyal-love-god/.

Bloom, Jon. "The Secret to Breaking Free from Habitual Sin." *Desiring God* (June 29, 2019), https://www.desiringgod.org/articles/the-secret-to-breaking-free-from-habitual-sin.

Bowlby, John. "Attachment." *Attachment and Loss*. Vol. 1. New York: Basic Books, 1982.

Carson, D. A. "A Little Introduction to Covenants." *Desiring God* (November 4, 2016), https://www.desiringgod.org/interviews/a-little-introduction-to-covenants.

Chen, Annie. *The Attachment Theory Workbook: Powerful Tools to Promote Understanding, Increase Stability, and Build Lasting Relationships*. Naperville, IL: Callisto Publishing LLC, 2019.

Daily Grace Co. *The Bible Themes Handbook*. Spring, TX: The Daily Grace Co., 2022.

Davis, Shirley. "The Tragedy of Never Feeling Safe." *CPTSD Foundation* (June 27, 2022), https://cptsdfoundation.org/2022/06/27/the-tragedy-of-never-feeling-safe/.

Dodson, Julie. "Object Relations Theory Explained." *Better Help* (October 10, 2024), https://

www.betterhelp.com/advice/therapy/how-object-relations-therapy-can-help-your-relationship/.

Ellison, Christopher G., Matt Bradshaw, Kevin J. Flannelly, and Kathleen C. Galek. "Prayer, Attachment to God, and Symptoms of Anxiety-Related Disorders Among U.S. Adults." *Sociology of Religion* 75, no. 2 (Summer 2014): 208–33.

Epstein, Sarah. "What is a Cycle-Breaker?" *Psychology Today* (July 15, 2022), https://www.psychologytoday.com/us/blog/between-the-generations/202207/what-is-cycle-breaker.

ESV Study Bible. Wheaton, IL: Crossway, 2008.

Ettenberger, Mark, Łucja Bieleninik, Shulamit Epstein, and Cochavit Elefant. "Defining Attachment and Bonding: Overlaps, Differences and Implications for Music Therapy Clinical Practice and Research in the Neonatal Intensive Care Unit (NICU)." *International Journal of Environmental Research and Public Health* (February 10, 2021), https://www.ncbi.nlm.nih.gov/pmc/articles/PMC7916808/#:~:text=Attachment%20theory%20describes%20essentially%20how,the%20early%20parent–infant%20relationship.

Fritscher, Lisa. "Understanding Fear of Abandonment," *Verywell Mind* (July 1, 2024), https://www.verywellmind.com/fear-of-abandonment-2671741.

Fyall, Bob. *ESV Expository Commentary: Isaiah–Ezekiel*, Vol. 6. Wheaton, IL: Crossway, 2022.

Gibson, Lindsay C. *Adult Children of Emotionally Immature Parents: How to Heal from Distant, Rejecting, or Self-Involved Parents*. Oakland, CA: New Harbinger Publications, 2015.

Gibson, Lindsay C. *Recovering from Emotionally Immature Parents: Practical Tools to Establish Boundaries and Reclaim Your Emotional Autonomy*. Oakland, CA: New Harbinger Publications, 2019.

Goleman, Daniel. "John Bowlby, Psychiatric Pioneer on Mother-Child Bond, Dies at 83." *New York Times* (September 14, 1990), https://www.nytimes.com/1990/09/14/obituaries/john-bowlby-psychiatric-pioneer-on-mother-child-bond-dies-at-83.html.

History.com editors. "ISIS." *History Channel* (June 7, 2019), https://www.history.com/topics/.21st-century/isis.

Kübler-Ross, Elizabeth and David Kessler. *On Grief & Grieving: Finding the Meaning of Grief Through the Five Stages of Loss*. New York: Scribner, 2005.

Lewis, C. S. *A Grief Observed*. San Francisco: HarperOne, 2015.

Marks, Gene. "These Handsome Men Get Paid to Make Women Cry." *Washington Post* (January 17, 2018), https://www.washingtonpost.com/news/on-small-business/wp/2018/01/17/these-handsome-men-get-paid-to-make-women-cry/.

Mathis, David. "To Groan is Human—and Christian." *Desiring God* (November 13, 2022), https://www.desiringgod.org/articles/to-groan-is-human-and-christian.

MediLodge, "What is Wound Care and What to Expect During This Treatment." https://medilodge.com/announcement/

what-is-wound-care-and-what-to-expect-during-this-treatment/.

Merriam-Webster.com Dictionary. https://www.merriam-webster.com.

Newhouse, Leo. "Is Crying Good for You?" *Harvard Health Blog* (March 1, 2021), https://www.health.harvard.edu/blog/is-crying-good-for-you-2021030122020.

Newport Institute. "Fear of Abandonment in Young Adults: What It Means and How to Heal" (July 17, 2023), https://www.newportinstitute.com/resources/mental-health/fear-of-abandonment/.

Ortlund, Dane. *ESV Expository Commentary: Romans–Galatians.* Wheaton, IL: Crossway, 2020.

Oxford English Dictionary. https://www.oed.com.

Patterson, Dorothy Kelley and Rhonda Harrington Kelley, eds. *Women's Evangelical Commentary: Old Testament.* Nashville: Holman Reference Publishers, 2011.

Perry, Bruce and Oprah Winfrey. *What Happened to You?: Conversations on Trauma, Resilience, and Healing.* New York: Flatiron Books, 2021.

Piper, John. "What is Love?" *Desiring God* (July 28, 2015), https://www.desiringgod.org/interviews/what-is-love.

Poole Heller, Diane. *The Power of Attachment: How to Create Deep and Lasting Intimate Relationships.* Boulder, CO: Sounds True, 2019.

Smith, Steven. *Christ-Centered Exposition: Exalting Jesus in Jeremiah and Lamentations.* Nashville: Holman Bible Publishers, 2019.

Spurgeon, Charles Haddon. "A Woman of a Sorrowful Spirit." The Spurgeon Center for Biblical Preaching at Midwestern Seminary, https://www.spurgeon.org/resource-library/sermons/a-woman-of-a-sorrowful-spirit/#flipbook/.

Spurgeon, Charles Haddon. "Cries from the Cross." The Spurgeon Center for Biblical Preaching at Midwestern Seminary (November 2, 1856), https://www.spurgeon.org/resource-library/sermons/cries-from-the-cross/#flipbook/.

Spurgeon, Charles Haddon. "The Covenant Pleaded, No. 1451B: A Sermon Delivered by C. H. Spurgeon, at the Metropolitan Tabernacle, Newington." *Spurgeon Gems*, Chapel Library (2019). http://www.spurgeongems.org/sermon/chs1451B.pdf.

Spurgeon, Charles Haddon. "Repentance After Conversion." The Spurgeon Center for Biblical Preaching at Midwestern Seminary (June 12, 1887), https://www.spurgeon.org/resource-library/sermons/repentance-after-conversion/#flipbook/.

Spurgeon, Charles Haddon. "Psalm 42." *The Treasury of David.* New York: Funk & Wagnalls, 1883.

Stines, Sharie. "Emotional Abandonment and Threats of Abuse." *Psych Central* (December 20, 2017), https://psychcentral.com/pro/recovery-expert/2017/12/emotional-abuse-and-threats-of-abandonment#4.

Storms, Sam. "1 Peter." *ESV Expository Commentary: Hebrews-Revelation*. ed. Iain M. Duguid. Wheaton, IL: Crossway, 2018.

Strauss Cohen, Ilene. "Family Relationship Patterns." *Psychology Today* (April 15, 2024), https://www.psychologytoday.com/us/blog/your-emotional-meter/202404/family-relationship-patterns#:~:text=Families%20pass%20on%20behaviors%2C%20emotions,continue%20and%20which%20to%20change.

Survivors of Bereavement by Suicide. "For Professionals" (2024), https://uksobs.org/for-professionals/how-suicide-bereavement-is-different.

Thompson, Curt. *Anatomy of the Soul: Surprising Connections Between Neuroscience and Spiritual Practices That Can Transform Your Life and Relationships*. Carol Stream, IL: Tyndale Momentum, 2010.

Thompson, Curt. *The Soul of Shame: Retelling the Stories We Believe About Ourselves*. Lisle, IL: IVP Press, 2015.

Tozer, A. W. *The Knowledge of the Holy*. San Francisco: HarperOne, 2009.

Van Neste, Ray. "1, 2, and 3 John." *ESV Expository Commentary: Hebrews-Revelation.*, ed. Iain M. Duguid. Wheaton, IL: Crossway, 2018.

Wenham, Gordon J. *Word Biblical Commentary: Genesis 1–15*. Grand Rapids, MI: Zondervan Academic, 2014.

West, Colleen. *We All Have Parts: An Illustrated Guide to Healing Trauma with Internal Family Systems*. Eau Claire, WI: PESI Publishing, 2021.

Woolard, Whitney. "The Five Key Covenants God Made with Humans in the Bible." *The Bible Project* (April 3, 2018), https://bibleproject.com/articles/covenants-the-backbone-bible/.

Zodhiates, Spiros, ed. *The Complete Word Study Dictionary: New Testament*. Electronic edition. AMG Publishers, 2000.

Notes

Introduction

1. *Merriam-Webster*, s.v. "lament," accessed January 6, 2024, https://www.merriam-webster.com/dictionary/lament.

Chapter 1

1. *Merriam-Webs*ter, s.v. "grief," accessed January 8, 2024, https://www.merriam-webster.com/dictionary/grief.

2. Maria Shriver, foreword to *On Grief & Grieving: Finding the Meaning of Grief Through the Five Stages of Loss* by Elizabeth Kübler-Ross and David Kessler (Scribner, 2005), xiv–xv.

3. Kübler-Ross and Kessler, *On Grief & Grieving*, xxi.

4. Kubler-Ross and Kessler, *On Grief & Grieving*, 1.

5. Madeleine L'Engle, foreword to *A Grief Observed* by C. S. Lewis (HarperOne, 2015), 6.

6. Kubler-Ross and Kessler, *On Grief & Grieving*, 7.

7. Kubler-Ross and Kessler, *On Grief & Grieving*, 8.

8. American Psychiatric Association, *Diagnostic and Statistical Manual of Mental Disorders*, 5th ed., text revision (American Psychiatric Association Publishing, 2022), 324–25.

9. Survivors of Bereavement by Suicide, "For Professionals" (2024), accessed January 8, 2024, https://uksobs.org/for-professionals/how-suicide-bereavement-is-different/?doing_wp_cron=1703254255.9464759826660156250000.

10. American Psychiatric Association, *Diagnostic and Statistical Manual of Mental Disorders*, 325.

Chapter 2

1. *Oxford English Dictionary*, s.v. "lament (n.)," July 2023, https://doi.org/10.1093/OED/5576149127.
2. *ESV Study Bible* (Crossway, 2008), 939.
3. *ESV Study Bible*, 953.
4. Charles Haddon Spurgeon, "A Woman of a Sorrowful Spirit" (The Spurgeon Center for Biblical Preaching at Midwestern Seminary, 1970), accessed May 4, 2024, https://www.spurgeon.org/resource-library/sermons/a-woman-of-a-sorrowful-spirit/#flipbook/.
5. *ESV Study Bible*, 1048.

Chapter 3

1. Dan B. Allender and Tremper Longman II, *The Cry of the Soul: How Our Emotions Reveal Our Deepest Questions About God* (NavPress, 2015), 28.
2. Charles H. Spurgeon, "Psalm 42," *The Treasury of David* (Funk & Wagnalls, 1883), 272.

Chapter 4

1. Lindsay C. Gibson, *Adult Children of Emotionally Immature Parents: How to Heal from Distant, Rejecting, or Self-Involved Parents* (New Harbinger Publications, 2015), 1.
2. Gibson, *Adult Children of Emotionally Immature Parents*, 7–8.
3. Bruce D. Perry and Oprah Winfrey, *What Happened to You?: Conversations on Trauma, Resilience, and Healing* (Flatiron Books, 2021), 287.
4. Gibson, *Adult Children of Emotionally Immature Parents*, 45.

5. Gibson, *Adult Children of Emotionally Immature Parents*, 171.
6. Warren Baker and Eugene Carpenter, eds., *The Complete Word Study Dictionary: Old Testament* (AMG Publishers, 2003), 128.
7. Shirley Davis, "The Tragedy of Never Feeling Safe," cptsdfoundation.org, 2022, accessed February 20, 2024, https://cptsdfoundation.org/2022/06/27/the-tragedy-of-never-feeling-safe/.
8. Curt Thompson, *Anatomy of the Soul: Surprising Connections Between Neuroscience and Spiritual Practices That Can Transform Your Life and Relationships* (Tyndale Momentum, 2010), 13.
9. Lindsay C. Gibson, *Recovering from Emotionally Immature Parents: Practical Tools to Establish Boundaries and Reclaim Your Emotional Autonomy* (New Harbinger Publications, 2019), 28.
10. Curt Thompson, *The Soul of Shame: Retelling the Stories We Believe About Ourselves* (IVP Press, 2015), 28.
11. Gibson, *Adult Children of Emotionally Immature Parents*, 185.

Chapter 5

1. John Bowlby, "Attachment," *Attachment and Loss, vol. 1* (Basic Books, 1982), 195.
2. Annie Chen, *The Attachment Theory Workbook: Powerful Tools to Promote Understanding, Increase Stability, and Build Lasting Relationships* (Callisto Publishing LLC, 2019), 85.
3. Mark Ettenberger et al., "Defining Attachment and Bonding: Overlaps, Differences and Implications for Music Therapy Clinical Practice and Research in the Neonatal Intensive Care Unit (NICU)," *International Journal of Environmental Research and Public Health*, February 10, 2021, accessed July 8, 2024, https://www.ncbi.nlm.nih.gov/pmc/articles/PMC7916808/#:~:text=Attachment%20theory%20describes%20essentially%20how,the%20early%20parent–infant%20relationship.

4. Bob Fyall, "Isaiah 49:15," *ESV Expository Commentary: Isaiah–Ezekiel*, vol. 6 (Crossway, 2022).

5. Diane Poole Heller, *The Power of Attachment: How to Create Deep and Lasting Intimate Relationships* (Sounds True, 2019), 27.

6. Chen, *The Attachment Theory Workbook*, 85.

7. Christopher G. Ellison et al., "Prayer, Attachment to God, and Symptoms of Anxiety-Related Disorders Among U.S. Adults," *Sociology of Religion* 75, no. 2 (Summer 2014): 208, https://www.baylorisr.org/wp-content/uploads/Sociology-of-Religion-2014-Ellison-208-33.pdf.

8. Ellison et al., "Prayer, Attachment to God, and Symptoms of Anxiety-Related Disorders Among U.S. Adults," 226, https://www.baylorisr.org/wp-content/uploads/Sociology-of-Religion-2014-Ellison-208-33.pdf.

9. Ellison et al., "Prayer, Attachment to God, and Symptoms of Anxiety-Related Disorders Among U.S. Adults," 226, https://www.baylorisr.org/wp-content/uploads/Sociology-of-Religion-2014-Ellison-208-33.pdf.

10. Poole Heller, *The Power of Attachment*, 46–47.

11. Curt Thompson, *Anatomy of the Soul: Surprising Connections Between Neuroscience and Spiritual Practices That Can Transform Your Life and Relationships* (Tyndale Momentum, 2010), 136.

12. Poole Heller, *The Power of Attachment*, 10.

Chapter 6

1. *Merriam-Webster*, s.v. "abandon," accessed March 3, 2024, https://www.merriam-webster.com/dictionary/abandon.

2. Sharie Stines, "Emotional Abandonment and Threats of Abuse," *Psych Central*, accessed March 17, 2024, https://psychcentral.com/pro/recovery-expert/2017/12/emotional-abuse-and-threats-of-abandonment#4.

3. Ray Van Neste, "1 John 4:13–21," *ESV Expository Commentary* (Crossway, 2018), 238.

4. Bruce D. Perry and Oprah Winfrey, *What Happened to You?: Conversations on Trauma, Resilience, and Healing* (Flatiron Books, 2021), 77.

5. John Piper, "What is Love?" *Desiring God* (July 28, 2015), accessed August 5, 2024, https://www.desiringgod.org/interviews/what-is-love.

6. A. W. Tozer, *The Knowledge of the Holy* (HarperOne, 2009), 69.

7. Curt Thompson, *The Soul of Shame: Retelling the Stories We Believe About Ourselves* (IVP Press, 2015), 72.

8. Lisa Fritscher, "Understanding Fear of Abandonment," *Verywell Mind* (July 1, 2024), accessed June 23, 2025, https://www.verywellmind.com/fear-of-abandonment-2671741.

9. Ilene Strauss Cohen, "Family Relationship Patterns," *Psychology Today* (April 15, 2024), accessed August 3, 2024, https://www.psychologytoday.com/us/blog/your-emotional-meter/202404/family-relationship-patterns#:~:text=Families%20pass%20on%20behaviors%2C%20emotions,continue%20and%20which%20to%20change.

10. Sam Storms, "1 Peter 1:13–2:3," *ESV Expository Commentary* (Crossway, 2018), 160.

11. Julie Dodson, "Object Relations Theory Explained," *Better Help* (October 10, 2024), accessed July 19, 2024, https://www.betterhelp.com/advice/therapy/how-object-relations-therapy-can-help-your-relationship.

12. "Fear of Abandonment in Young Adults: What It Means and How to Heal," *Newport Institute* (July 17, 2023), accessed July 30, 2024, https://www.newportinstitute.com/resources/mental-health/fear-of-abandonment.

13. Steven Smith, *Christ-Centered Exposition: Exalting Jesus in Jeremiah and Lamentations* (Holman Bible Publishers, 2019), 263.

14. Charles Haddon Spurgeon, "Cries from the Cross," The Spurgeon Center for Biblical Preaching at Midwestern Seminary, accessed August 8, 2024, https://www.spurgeon.org/resource-library/sermons/cries-from-the-cross/#flipbook/.

15. Dorothy Kelley Patterson and Rhonda Harrington Kelley, eds. *Women's Evangelical Commentary: Old Testament* (Holman Reference Publishers, 2011), 1237.

16. Warren Baker and Eugene Carpenter, eds. *The Complete Word Study Dictionary: Old Testament* (AMG Publishers, 2003), 1083.

Chapter 7

1. Charles Spurgeon, "The Covenant Pleaded, No. 1451B: A Sermon Delivered by C. H. Spurgeon, at the Metropolitan Tabernacle, Newington." *Spurgeon Gems*, Chapel Library (2019), http://www.spurgeongems.org/sermon/chs1451B.pdf.

2. D. A. Carson, "A Little Introduction to Covenants," *Desiring God* (November 4, 2016), accessed August 15, 2024, https://www.desiringgod.org/interviews/a-little-introduction-to-covenants.

3. Whitney Woolard, "The Five Key Covenants God Made with Humans in the Bible," *The Bible Project* (April 3, 2018), accessed August 19, 2024, https://bibleproject.com/articles/covenants-the-backbone-bible/.

4. Gordon J. Wenham, *Word Biblical Commentary: Genesis 1–15* (Zondervan Academic, 2014), 548.

5. Daily Grace Co., *The Bible Themes Handbook* (The Daily Grace Co., 2022), 15–16.

6. Warren Baker and Eugene Carpenter, eds., *The Complete Word Study Dictionary: Old Testa*ment (AMG Publishers, 2003), 360.

7. "The Loyal Love of God," Bible Project (November 2, 2020), accessed August 20, 2024, https://bibleproject.com/podcast/loyal-love-god/.

8. Daily Grace Co., *The Bible Themes Handbook*, 9.

Chapter 8

1. Sarah Epstein, "What is a Cycle-Breaker?" *Psychology Today* (July 15, 2022), accessed June 28, 2024, https://www.psychologytoday.com/us/blog/between-the-generations/202207/what-is-cycle-breaker.

2. Bruce Perry and Oprah Winfrey, *What Happened to You?: Conversations on Trauma, Resilience, and Healing* (Flatiron Books, 2021), 82.

3. Perry and Winfrey, *What Happened to You?*, 76.

4. Perry and Winfrey, *What Happened to You?*, 76.

5. Perry and Winfrey, *What Happened to You?*, 162.

6. MediLodge, "What is Wound Care and What to Expect During This Treatment," accessed June 14, 2024, https://medilodge.com/announcement/what-is-wound-care-and-what-to-expect-during-this-treatment/.

7. Dorothy Kelley Patterson and Rhonda Harrington Kelley, eds., *Women's Evangelical Commentary: Old Testament* (Holman Reference Publishers, 2011), 317.

8. Epstein, "What is a Cycle-Breaker?"

9. Perry and Winfrey, *What Happened to You?*, 183.

Chapter 9

1. Arthur Bennett, ed., *The Valley of Vision: A Collection of Puritan Prayers and Devotions* (The Banner of Truth Trust, 1988), xv.

2. Jon Bloom, "The Secret to Breaking Free from Habitual Sin," *Desiring God* (June 29, 2019), https://www.desiringgod.org/articles/the-secret-to-breaking-free-from-habitual-sin.

3. Colleen West, *We All Have Parts: An Illustrated Guide to Healing Trauma with Internal Family Systems* (PESI Publishing, 2021), 17. Internal Family Systems is a type of therapy founded by Richard C. Schwartz, PhD.

4. West, *We All Have Parts*, 24.

5. Spiros Zodhiates, ed., "Metamélomai," *The Complete Word Study Dictionary: New Testament*, electronic ed. (AMG Publishers, 2000).

6. *ESV Study Bible* (Crossway, 2008), 999.

7. Charles Haddon Spurgeon, "Repentance After Conversion," The Spurgeon Center for Biblical Preaching at Midwestern Seminary, June 12, 1887, accessed January 9, 2024, https://www.spurgeon.org/resource-library/sermons/repentance-after-conversion/#flipbook/.

8. Dane Ortlund, *ESV Expository Commentary: Romans–Galatians* (Crossway, 2020), 272.

Chapter 10

1. Alexandra Benisek, "Why We Cry: The Truth About Tearing Up," *WebMD* (November 23, 2024), accessed August 25, 2024, https://www.webmd.com/balance/why-we-cry-tearing-up.

2. Leo Newhouse, "Is Crying Good for You?" *Harvard Health Blog* (March 1, 2021), accessed August 25, 2024, https://www.health.harvard.edu/blog/is-crying-good-for-you-2021030122020.

3. Gene Marks, "These Handsome Men Get Paid to Make Women Cry," *Washington Post* (January 17, 2018), accessed August 25, 2024, https://www.washingtonpost.com/news/on-small-business/wp/2018/01/17/these-handsome-men-get-paid-to-make-women-cry/.

4. "Psychotherapy: Understanding Group Therapy," *American Psychological Association* (October 31, 2019), accessed August 27, 2024, https://www.apa.org/topics/psychotherapy/group-therapy.

5. Dane Ortlund, *ESV Expository Commentary: Romans–Galatians* (Crossway, 2020), 189.

6. *ESV Study Bible* (Crossway, 2008), 1042.

7. Bruce Perry and Oprah Winfrey, *What Happened to You?: Conversations on Trauma, Resilience, and Healing* (Flatiron Books, 2021), 75.

8. David Mathis, "To Groan is Human—and Christian," *Desiring God* (November 13, 2022), accessed September 3, 2024, https://www.desiringgod.org/articles/to-groan-is-human-and-christian.

Chapter 11

1. *ESV Study Bible* (Crossway, 2008), 374.

2. Spiros Zodhiates, *The Complete Word Study Dictionary: New Testament* (AMG Publishers, 1992).

3. History.com editors, "ISIS," *History Channel* (June 7, 2019), accessed May 20, 2024, https://www.history.com/topics/.21st-century/isis.

4. *ESV Study Bible*, 1863.

Epilogue

1. *ESV Study Bible* (Crossway, 2008), 543.